The Lustral Waters

John 3 and 19

Mystery, Majesty and Mathematics in John's Gospel #3

Anne Hamilton

The Lustral Waters—John 3 and 19:
Mystery, Majesty and Mathematics in John's Gospel #3

© Anne Hamilton 2025
Published by Armour Books
P. O. Box 492, Corinda QLD 4075 Australia

Cover & interior design and typeset by Beckon Creative

Cover image composite: Lucky Girl Creative © 2020, Cottage Arts © 2019,
   Seatrout Scraps © 2017, Creative Memories © 2010, Forever Artisan 6 © 2024
   courtesy of Forever.com; Lightstock | Ben White, 'water in cupped hands of Jesus'
Part 1: Unsplash | Sardar Faizan 'the sun is setting behind the clouds in the sky',
   Hermansyah 'aerial photo of body of water during daytime';
   water texture Forever.com
Part 2: Depositphotos | urfingus 'hourglass with dripping water close up,
   time concept', dejtan05 'Small porcelain vase closeup on black and white
   bacckgrounde'; Unsplash | Sime Basioli, Photoholgic
Part 3: Lightstock | PhotoGranary 'Moses holds out his staff. Parted Seas.';
   Unsplash | Passadori 'Brown wooden surface'
Part 4: Lightstock | Kevin Carden 'empty tomb', Pearl 'Jesus crucified at sunset';
   Unsplash | Jack Hunter
Part 5: Lucky Girl Creative © 2020, 2024/ Forever Artisan 6 © 2024;
   Creative Fabrica | Drumpee Design; Etsy | Nightingale Craftery
Part 6: Depositphotos | zeferli@gmail.com 'Low key image of Jewish holiday
Hanukkah', Hasenonkel 'The hot burning contour of a menorah';
   iStock | lilly3 'Ancient Game of Dice'
Part 7: Unsplash | Maria Orlova;
   Depositphotos | RuslanKal, 'Waterfall Banias landscape'
Part 8: Depositphotos | sergeypeterman 'Water splash isolated on white',
   kevron2002 'A big storm and tornado on top of the pages of a Bible with a bright
   lighthouse'; iStock | artplus 'The inversion of the crown of thorns and the crown'
All other artwork: Beckon Creative

ISBN: 978-1-925380-76-7

 A catalogue record for this book is available from the National Library of Australia

All rights reserved. No part of this publication may be reproduced, stored in, or introduced into a retrieval system, or transmitted, in any form, or by any means (electronic, mechanical, photocopying, recording or otherwise) without the prior written permission of the publisher.

Note: Australian spelling and grammar conventions are used throughout this book.

The Lustral Waters

Anne Hamilton

Unless otherwise noted, Scripture quotations are taken from The Holy Bible, Berean Study Bible, BSB Copyright ©2016 by Bible Hub Used by Permission. All Rights Reserved Worldwide.

Scripture quotations marked BLB are taken from the The Blue Letter Bible. Used by permission. blueletterbible.org

Scripture quotations marked BSB are taken from the The Holy Bible, Berean Study Bible, BSB Copyright ©2016 by Bible Hub Used by Permission. All Rights Reserved Worldwide.

Scripture quotations marked CEV are from the Contemporary English Version Copyright © 1991, 1992, 1995 by American Bible Society. Used by Permission.

Scripture quotations marked ESV are taken from the ESV® Bible (The Holy Bible, English Standard Version®), copyright © 2001 by Crossway, a publishing ministry of Good News Publishers. Used by permission. All rights reserved.

Scripture quotations marked GWT are taken from GOD'S WORD®, a copyrighted work of God's Word to the Nations. Quotations are used by permission. Copyright 1995 by God's Word to the Nations. All rights reserved.

Scripture quotations marked ISV are taken from the Holy Bible: International Standard Version®. Copyright © 1996-forever by The ISV Foundation. ALL RIGHTS RESERVED INTERNATIONALLY. Used by permission.

Scripture quotations marked KJV are taken from the King James Version of the Bible. Public domain.

Scripture quotations marked NASB are taken from the New American Standard Bible®, Copyright © 1960, 1962, 1963, 1968, 1971, 1972, 1973, 1975, 1977, 1995 by The Lockman Foundation. Used by permission. (www.Lockman.org)

Scripture quotations designated NET are from the NET Bible® copyright ©1996-2016 by Biblical Studies Press, L.L.C. http://netbible.com Scripture quoted by permission. All rights reserved.

Scripture quotations marked NLT are taken from the Holy Bible, New Living Translation, copyright 1996, 2004. Used by permission of Tyndale House Publishers, Inc., Wheaton, Illinois 60189. All rights reserved.

Scripture quotations marked NIV are taken from the Holy Bible, New International Version®, NIV®. Copyright © 1973, 1978, 1984, 2011 by Biblica, Inc.™ Used by permission of Zondervan. All rights reserved worldwide. www.zondervan.com The "NIV" and "New International Version" are trademarks registered in the United States Patent and Trademark Office by Biblica, Inc.™.

Scripture quotations marked NKJV are taken from the New King James Version. Copyright © 1982 by Thomas Nelson, Inc. Used by permission. All rights reserved.

Scripture quotations marked NRS are taken from New Revised Standard Version of the Bible, copyright 1952 [2nd edition, 1971] by the Division of Christian Education of the National Council of the Churches of Christ in the United States of America. Used by permission. All rights reserved.

Dedication

With many thanks:

Rebekah

Judy

Ruth

Edgar

Mark

Jenny

Table of Contents

	Introduction	9
Part 1		12
1.1	Beyond Jerusalem	15
1.2	Recapitulation	20
1.3	Ephesian Artemis	23
1.4	Ephesian Grammata	26
1.5	John and Jonah	29
1.6	Chiasmus	35
Part 2		38
2.1	Man of the Breakthrough	41
2.2	Wordplay	46
2.3	A Visitor by Night	49
2.4	Visitors from the East	51
2.5	The Mountain of Spices	55
2.6	The New Samuel	58
2.7	According to Jewish Burial Custom	66
2.8	Symphony of Names	70
Part 3		76
3.1	Birth of the Bride	79
3.2	The Kingdom of God	83
3.3	Testimony and Belief	85
3.4	The Breath of the Spirit	88
3.5	The 'Twice-born'	91
Part 4		94
4.1	Ascent and Descent	97
4.2	Lifted Up	100
4.3	The Highway of Angels	103

4.4	Drawing Water	106
4.5	Nicodemus in the War with Rome	115
4.6	Eternal Life	119
4.7	Compunction	124
4.8	Archimedes	127
4.9	Into the Curse	132

Part 5 — 138

5.1	The Doorposts of Belief	141
5.2	The Thirst of the Living Water	145
5.3	The Bridegroom Speaks	147
5.4	Everyone Who Believes	149
5.5	Everyone Who Doesn't Believe	151

Part 6 — 154

6.1	Light and Lots	157
6.2	Gambling Responsibly	160
6.3	Light of Life	163
6.4	Mother and Son	166
6.5	Reuben's Mantle	172
6.6	The Tree of Weeping	177
6.7	Aenon near Salim	180

Part 7 — 186

7.1	A Dispute about Ceremonial Washing	189
7.2	The Place of the Skull	193
7.3	Adversaries	201
7.4	Mathematically Rolled Away	204
7.5	The King's Crown	209
7.6	The Bridegroom's Crown	212
7.7	The Bride's Mikvah	214
7.8	The 'Invincible Sun'	217
7.9	The King of the Jews	224

Part 8 — 228

8.1	Earthly and Heavenly	231
8.2	Rejection	237
8.3	Living and Lustral	242

	Appendix 1	245
	Appendix 2	247

Map Galilee 42

INTRODUCTION

JOHN'S GOSPEL IS AN EPIC POEM. I can say that with supreme confidence because by the end of the third chapter we're 112 verses into the text, and there's not a single verse without a chiastic match at the end.

I say I've found 'a' match and not 'the' match in each case because I think the vast majority of them are not simple correspondences but highly complex, richly textured, and profoundly structured in their parallelisms. I'm sure I have not exhausted the treasure trove of allusions in each pair or their links to adjacent scenes but I have found some form of conceptual link in every case.

It's been tough at times. I've struggled to follow John's thoughts, wondering for instance how the verdict of the Light could in any way be related to the casting of lots for Jesus' clothes. There have been many other similar puzzles. Generally speaking, I've come to the conclusion that the easiest approach to a conundrum is to remember that John is a Jew writing in Greek but thinking in Hebrew. Thus it's wise to look straight away for Hebrew words that embody the various concepts of a particular passage.

Once again, although there's an exact chapter examined at the front, it's not the case at the back. Despite the subtitle of the book, *John 3 and 19*, it's really 3 and 19:13–41.

Generally speaking, except where there's new information and insight I've come across, I have not gone over the details in the previous books to a great depth. I have mentioned various conclusions from them as simple statements or occasionally in brief summaries. As a consequence of this, the first section is dense with abridged conclusions from the previous volumes in this series. Much of this will likely be very surprising, since it comes directly from the chiastic parallels. So, to examine the full evidence for some of my more unusual declarations, particularly in the opening section, please look into the relevant book.

As usual, this book is designed using what MJJ Menken[1] and J Smit Sibinga[2] call 'numerical literary style'. In tribute to John's own mathematical structure I have embedded my text in sections with their own numerical design and symbolism. Mine is nowhere near as complex and rich as his, and it's my hope that, as you are reading, you won't even notice the arithmetic underlay. But it's there: sometimes 490 (seventy times seven) for *forgiveness*; sometimes 496 for *Immanuel*; sometimes 618 and 1000 and 1618 for the *logos*; sometimes 1111 for *covenant*; sometimes 1010 for *divine sustenance*; sometimes 777 for the *Armour of God* or *His Kiss*.

Unfortunately, Menken's mathematical analysis of the Greek text of John's gospel does not include the third or third last chapter. There are several text variations that would have made such a project very difficult at the level of his investigations which included word, letter, syllable and stressed syllable counts. However, by restricting myself to word counts and ignoring spelling variations, I simplified the process. This has enabled an examination of both the repeating patterns in the mathematical

---

[1] Author of *Numerical Literary Techniques in John: The Fourth Evangelist's Use of Numbers of Words and Syllables* (Novum Testamentum, Supplements), Brill 1985

[2] Author of *1 Cor. 15:8/9 and Other Divisions in 1 Cor. 15:1-11*, Novum Testamentum Vol. 39, Fasc. 1 (Jan., 1997), Brill

architecture and also the interaction between the numbers and the wording.

Following on from the discovery outlined in the previous books in this series that the stories John presents to us identify the passing of various mantles via the parallelisms of the first and last chapters, as well as the second and second-last chapters, it's natural to wonder if there is yet another mantle highlighted in the third and third-last chapters. John's first and last chapters record the passing on of a prophetic mantle by Jesus, and those in the second and second-last chapters describe the granting of a mantle of restorative justice. These legacies—one coming down from Elijah and one from Joseph—are bestowed in surprising ways. Yet we shouldn't be surprised that our own cultural expectations are shattered by God's grace.

In John's third chapter and its corresponding partner, two mantles are passed on by Jesus: one belonged to Moses and the other to Reuben, the firstborn of Jacob's sons.

It's a matter of becoming sensitised to John's record of the various individual bequests Jesus passed to His disciples as an inheritance. A mantle, significantly, was not given for His followers to repeat the works of those who wore it before them; it was given for them to complete it.

So it is for us. We too are given mantles, passed down the family of faith to us. And we too are called in the power and strength of the Holy Spirit to advance the assignment that comes with the mantle towards its ultimate fulfilment in Jesus.

Anne Hamilton

Seventeen Mile Rocks, Australia

March 2025

1.1 Beyond Jerusalem

Nearly forty years after Jesus ascended to heaven, Roman legions surrounded Jerusalem. As the armies advanced on the capital, many Christians remembered the Lord's warning and fled. A large contingent of them sought refuge in Pella, one of the ten cities of the Decapolis. In the early days of Jesus' ministry He had performed many miracles of healing throughout the region. Pella was situated on the east bank of the Jordan river about thirty kilometres[3] south of the Sea of Galilee and, as a result of the influx of refugees from Jerusalem, it became a Jewish-Christian hub. It is reputed to be the site of the earliest Christian churches.

Some historians dispute the 'flight to Pella', arguing that it is such an obscure locality there seems to be no good reason for Christians to have headed there for sanctuary. Surely believers would have preferred better-known cities. But Pella would have held a singular attraction for first century Christians. It was the closest town to Bethany-beyond-the-Jordan—the baptismal site where John the Baptiser began his ministry before he moved to Aenon near Salim.[4] In the rock pools of the ravine whose waters splashed out into the Jordan, John had immersed penitent pilgrims in the waters of baptism. It was here that, long before

---

3   Twenty miles.
4   John 3:23

John came on the scene, Elijah had hidden from King Ahab. For this was the Brook Cherith,[5] a place of refuge and provision in time of trouble. It was here that Jesus was baptised; it was here too that He retreated to spend the last winter of His life after He received death threats from the leaders in Jerusalem; it was here He received the news of Lazarus' illness.

Despite the doubts of some historians, Pella was a perfectly logical place to flee. Its proximity to Bethany-beyond-the-Jordan is the key to their choice. If Bethany was a haven good enough for Elijah and good enough for Jesus, then it certainly would have seemed more than good enough for Christians who looked up and saw the fulfilment of prophecy in Jesus' words about the city surrounded by troops.

Did John the apostle join in the 'flight to Pella'? Not every believer did. Nicodemus, for example, must have remained until at least the beginning of the siege—this is according to the famous accounts concerning him in Jewish writings. Was Mary, the mother of Jesus, escorted to Pella? Her keeping, after all, had been entrusted to John during the crucifixion. So, if he went there, surely she would have accompanied him. We have no way of knowing what their movements were.

Perhaps, however, the opening of John's gospel, set as it is at Bethany-beyond-the-Jordan in the Brook Cherith, is an acknowledgment of the community at nearby Pella. Such a tribute, if that's its motivation, would have been an expression of gratitude to a people who kept the faith alive in a dark hour.

---

5   It is currently known as the Wadi al-Yabis or Wadi al-Rayyan in the Kingdom of Jordan. The Yabis stream flows out into the Jordan River almost opposite the archaeological site of Beit She'an in Israel on the opposite bank. The nearby Jordanian town, Ajloun, is an enclave in a Muslim-majority country that is still nearly 50% Christian.

Many Christians returned to Jerusalem from Pella after the Roman war was over. Once again, John's movements are unknown. At some point, however, he moved north to Ephesus on the coast of the Ionian Sea. According to tradition, he took Mary with him.

At the time, Ephesus was one of the city-states of Greece, part of the Ionian League, under Roman control. Today, it is in the Izmir Province of Turkey.

The gospel had first been preached in Ephesus, probably in the early 50s, by Paul, Priscilla and Aquila. They had journeyed there together when Paul was en route from Corinth to Jerusalem. He continued on his journey and, while he was away, Apollos—a fervent supporter of the baptism of John—arrived. An eloquent defender of the need for repentance, Apollos was taken under Priscilla and Aquila's tutelage, and soon became a believer in Jesus. By the time Paul got back, Apollos had gone on to Corinth but the nucleus of a thriving Christian community had been established in Ephesus. Paul stayed there for two years, preaching daily in a lecture hall. Many healing miracles and exorcisms resulted from his ministry, and he was able to commission Timothy and Erastus as missionaries into Macedonia. His time in Ephesus came to an abrupt end with a riot.

The fame of the city of Ephesus had, for centuries, been built around the Temple of Artemis, one of the Seven Wonders of the Ancient World. Moreover, Ephesus was a major centre of magic. When some of its citizens turned to Christianity, they showed the sincerity of their repentance by publicly burning their scrolls of sorcery—valued at about 140 years' wages.[6]

Paul's activity increasingly threatened the livelihood of the silversmiths of Ephesus who made shrines and figurines of the

---

6   Acts 19:19

goddess, Ephesian Artemis. A metalworker named Demetrius stirred up a crowd, who seized Gaius and Aristarchus, the travelling companions of Paul, and hustled them to a theatre. Despite efforts to calm the assembly—most of whom, apparently, had no idea why they were there—they shouted for two hours, 'Great is Artemis of the Ephesians.'

The city clerk eventually managed to quell the uproar and dismissed the crowd. Paul said goodbye to the local church, then set out for Macedonia.[7]

This is the background into which John the apostle stepped. Ephesus had a vibrant Christian presence, yet was also a centre of idolatry whose businessmen were prepared to defend the 'genius loci', *the spirit of the place.*

Paul had, of course, written to the believers in Ephesus, and Timothy had ministered in the city. According to the early church historian Eusebius, Timothy was its first bishop and it's believed he was martyred there. And if the date for his death, 97 AD, is correct, then he would have known the apostle John.

In the last quarter of the first century, the rise of Gnosticism brought with it unique challenges to the Christian faith. Gnosticism is named from 'gnosis', *knowledge,* and its adherents claimed that salvation came, not through grace by faith, but through secret knowledge.[8]

---

7   Acts 1923–41
8   Gnosticism was not a unified system but a speculative religious belief. Teachers borrowed from Platonic philosophy, oriental mysticism, kabbalistic Judaism and Christianity. Gnosticism took many forms from gross immorality to a highly ethical life. One of the few characteristics that marked all Gnostics was their united attempt to come to God through their own reasoning and their rejection of the incarnation of Christ. See: Edgar Stubbersfield, *Ephesus: The Nursery of Christianity*, Wipf & Stock 2022

Ephesus, with its long-established culture of magic and sorcery, was a natural magnet for those attracted to the power of secret knowledge. Cerinthus, a Jew from Egypt and an early adherent to Gnosticism, was drawn there sometime in the 80s. John knew him. And perhaps we can be thankful for that. Otherwise, we might not have the fourth gospel. John was so appalled by the heresy Cerinthus was spreading throughout Asia Minor that, according to Irenaeus, he set out 'to remove that error which by Cerinthus had been disseminated among men.'[9]

The influence of the Nicolaitans[10] and Gnostics in Ephesus finally prompted John, late in life, to take up a pen and set the record straight.

---

9   Irenaeus, Bishop of Lugdunum, *Against Heresies (Book III, Chapter 11)*, newadvent.org/fathers/0103311.htm (accessed 11 July 2021) Irenaeus was a student of Polycarp who was mentored by John the apostle. See *The Elijah Tapestry: John 1 and 21*, the first book in this series, for more on Cerinthus and the Gnostics.

10 It's uncertain who the Nicolaitans were or what their teaching was; only that John was adamantly against it.

1.2 Recapitulation

THE BOOK OF THE WARS OF THE LORD is quoted in Numbers 21:14–15 where the border between the Amorites and the Moabites is briefly described. Apart from this tiny fragment, this ancient text has been completely lost.

Yet perhaps the gospel of John gives us strong hints about the contents of the Book of the Wars of the Lord. I suggest this for two reasons: first, because John is the one who presents Jesus to us as the War Messiah—using His long-expected title, the 'Son of Joseph'. Second, because John frames so much of his gospel in terms of extended recapitulation.

Recapitulation is the oldest theory of the atonement. This term was first used by Irenaeus, the same second-century bishop of Lyon who'd revealed that John's antagonism towards the Gnostics, and Cerinthus in particular, was the motivation for setting down his gospel. John had mentored Polycarp who had then gone on to teach Irenaeus.

By 'recapitulation', Irenaeus meant that Jesus had repaired the wounds of history. He had re-enacted the events leading up to the Fall, but had changed the outcome of the storyline in order to rectify Adam's sin.

Irenaeus borrowed the term 'recapitulation' from the art of rhetoric where it refers to the final summing up. The speaker marshals his arguments during the recapitulation, bringing them all together in a definitive conclusion. So 'recapitulation' means that, in Jesus, we see God's final word on the original transgression that brought death into the world and then cascaded into ever-increasing violence and evil. Jesus is therefore God's 'summary statement'—His Logos, His final rebuttal to the evil unleashed in the Garden of Eden.[11]

There's a symmetry to salvation history—not a perfect symmetry, because Jesus is at work mending and amending. Yet the summing up of all things in His work of redemption is apparent throughout John's gospel.[12]

However, the singular focus of Irenaeus and subsequent commentators on the atonement as a reversal of Adam's sin—and on the faithfulness of Mary compared to the faithlessness of Eve—obscures all the repair work Jesus performed *during His life*. To limit recapitulation to the crucifixion and resurrection misses the breathtaking splendour of the inversions and turnarounds Jesus accomplished during His ministry. As noted in the earlier books in this series, He didn't start the work of world-mending at the Cross and He didn't finish it there either. He was continually healing history. He was constantly remastering the plot of the events in the biblical chronicle, stitching up the wounds of the past and mending the ruptures in relationships across society that had existed for millennia.

In *The Summoning of Time* I pointed out how the symbolism of the miracle at Cana overturns the dispossession of the Egyptian people by Joseph—who'd inadvertently created a political

---

[11] See: https://www.theopedia.com/recapitulation-theory-of-atonement (accessed 27 January 2024)

[12] Jesus re-enacts or recapitulates the Fall so as to correct the erroneous actions of Adam. See: tmc.org.au (accessed 7 February 2024)

mechanism that was eventually used against the Israelites. In *The Elijah Tapestry*, I pointed out how Jesus set up the circumstances for the Gentiles to come into the Kingdom of God, an event that was apparently meant to begin in the time of Elijah.

These are recapitulations, no less than the reversal of the Eden story is. Yet behind each and every recapitulation is the conquest of one of the deities of the nations—and often several of them simultaneously. The scene with Mary the Magdalene, as a representative of mankind looking around a garden and asking where the Lord is, is an inversion of God looking around a garden for the first representatives of mankind and calling out, asking them where they were.

But there is so much more going on in that scene: it is an example of 'spolia opima', the complete stripping of an enemy commander of all the spoils of war. Jesus defeated the Canaanite deities—Baal-Hadad, Anat, Myrrh, Resheph—so comprehensively that nothing was left to them. He took back their titles, liturgies, legends, symbols and rituals, returning them all to their rightful owner, the Lord of heaven and earth.

Still, in an account where the inheritance Jesus passed to His disciples is such a significant theme, Anat the dispossessor is going to turn up several times in different guises. In Egypt she was Neith, in Greece Athena and, in Ephesus, she was of course Ephesian Artemis.

1.3 Ephesian Artemis

Artemis of the Greeks and Artemis of the Ephesians are, despite the similarity of their names, quite different. Yet, spiritually speaking, we can't entirely separate them. The first is the virgin goddess of the moon, a huntress who delights in the company of wild animals but is also a protector of children and a helper during childbirth. Ephesian Artemis, on the other hand, is associated with an urban setting rather than the wilderness. In fact, as the defender and patron of Ephesus, she was called 'saviour', 'lord' and 'queen of the cosmos'.[13]

Originally represented as a simple wood carving[14] draped in clothing and adorned with jewels, her image transitioned to a huntress figure before acquiring a multiplicity of breasts with bands of animals crossing her torso, signs of the zodiac around her neck and the Ephesian grammata on her mural[15] crown, girdle and feet. The band of animals indicated her title, 'Mistress of Beasts', the zodiac proclaimed her to be a higher authority than

---

[13] See: Edgar Stubbersfield, *Ephesus: The Nursery of Christianity*, Wipf & Stock 2022

[14] Such roughly hewn figures were called 'xoanon'.

[15] A mural crown features the walls of a city. This decoration proclaimed her the city's defender, and was similar to the crown of the dark mother goddess Cybele. Acts 19:35 refers to an image that fell from heaven. This is otherwise unknown for Artemis, but was associated with Cybele. It is therefore likely the worship of Artemis had merged with that of Cybele.

fate and appointed time, and the *grammata* demonstrated her role in magic.

Ephesian Artemis was often pictured in a doorway and may have had a helper role in crossing thresholds and making transitions. She was called 'Lysizones', *releaser of the girdle*, in reference to the girdle girls put on at puberty and removed after their first act of intercourse, dedicating it to the goddess. Married women were excluded from the temple of Artemis on penalty of death. There were statues of Amazons in the temple, as well as pan pipes to proclaim a woman's virginity. Women often served as priests in the Temple, including as high priests.

Edgar Stubbersfield describes the relationship between the goddess and her followers as being of a 'substance' nature. Her powers flowed to them like electricity and could be used as they wished. By reciting the myths, her followers called on her creative and sustaining powers. The myths were considered 'maps' which expressed the life-power of Ephesus.

There are many aspects of this description that align with the Canaanite goddess Anat—a bloodthirsty warmonger who was also considered to be a virgin huntress, but also strangely 'a mother of gods'.[16] The stars were said to be in her retinue,[17] she claims to rule over appointed time,[18] and at some times and places in Israelite history she was given the title 'Queen of Heaven'.[19]

---

16   Asherah is normally given this title.

17   Peter C. Craigie argued that the stars are part of Anat's retinue. See: Mark Smith and Wayne Pitard, *The Ugaritic Baal Cycle, Volume II. Introduction with Text, Translation and Commentary of KTU/CAT 1.3–1.4*, Vetus Testamentum, Supplements, Volume 114, Brill 2009

18   See Anne Hamilton, *Dealing with Lilith: Spirit of Dispossession, Strategies for the Threshold #10*, Armour Books 2024

19   She was worshipped under this title at Beit She'an during its occupation by the Egyptians. She may be the 'Queen of Heaven' mentioned by Jeremiah, since his hometown Anathoth was named after her.

As noted in *The Summoning of Time*, Anat is a hidden player in Israelite history. Her influence is profound. Yet if she is noticed at all—and that, unfortunately, occurs very rarely—she is completely underestimated. Nonetheless, she is responsible for the takedown of Elijah and his failure to complete his God-given assignment; she is the one who inspired Joseph to create the political mechanism that would eventually be used by the Egyptians to enslave his own people.

Her importance as a spiritual foe is shown during the very first ministry foray of Jesus. His actions in calling forward both ordinary and appointed time at the wedding feast of Cana to do His bidding are a direct attack against her. So too is His symbolic overturning of the dispossession she specialises in. By creating new wine—which, though it is fine and aged, is also undeniably 'new'—He promises a restoration of inheritance. The Hebrew word for *new wine* derives from *inheritance*.

John, according to the testimony of Irenaeus, wrote against the Gnostics and Nicolaitans. Yet I believe he also had Ephesian Artemis as a target. And so his stories of Jesus naturally focus on the nearest equivalent amongst the godlings who wanted to claim Israel, the land and people God had reserved for Himself, as their own turf. Chief amongst those deities were Baal-Hadad the Cloud-rider and his savage sister Anat. Her claims included the right to determine who should sit on the throne of heaven. She also asserted that she had brought about the elimination of Death and that she had the means to revivify the dead. Yes, pretty much anything Jesus could do, she could do better. That's what it amounted to. These were declarations that could not go unanswered.

Jesus made sure that each and every claim was struck down. And John made sure he recorded the stories where that happened.

1.4 Ephesian Grammata

The statue of Artemis in the temple at Ephesus had a series of words engraved on her crown and girdle as well as around her feet. These grammata were allegedly meaningless but were nevertheless seen as a protective force, providing the user could pronounce them correctly. There's an inherent contradiction in suggesting that nonsense needs to be babbled the right way in order to be infused with power, so many attempts were made to decode the grammata.

Like modern religious mantras, they were akin to 'stoicheion', *the ordered letters of the alphabet, the rudimentary sounds by which the universe was created,* or *heavenly spirits, astral beings* or *elementary principles that govern the minds of unbelievers.*

There were several different versions of the grammata. According to Plutarch, a priest of Apollo who served at the Delphic Oracle during the late first century and early second century, the magi counselled those who were demonically possessed to recite the Ephesian grammata. They were binding spells. Paul may well have been obliquely referring to them when he wrote:

> *As a* prisoner *for the Lord, then, I urge you to live a life worthy of the calling you have received.*
>
> Ephesians 4:1^{NIV}

The Greek word Paul uses here for *prisoner* refers to *binding* and can be interpreted as *binding with a magic spell*, as if he were held captive by enchantment.

The Ephesian grammata, these so-called meaningless words, were magic spells and arcane symbols that did not always need to be spoken to be effective. Athletes and warriors would bind them onto some part of their body in order to shackle their opponents. They became so famous they were banned in some games because of the advantage they were seen to give contestants wearing them.

Although the Ephesian grammata were said to be nonsense, ordinary grammata were of course weighty with meaning. It is the word from which we derive 'grammar', itself having a long association with magic. Originally referring to the art of letters—that is, to both philology and literature—grammar only came to mean the systematic rules for the usage of language in the sixteenth century. Before that, it could mean learning in general or a study of incantation and spells.

John twice uses the word 'grammata' in his gospel to refer to *writings* or *teachings*. Yet this is not in any way a reference to the Ephesian grammata. Rather he sets himself in opposition to that famous local export by his use of 'logos'. This term meaning *word, expression, reason*, or *ratio* with its Platonic overtones of ideal forms, as well as coherent mathematical and verbal communication, is in complete contrast to the Ephesian grammata.

The rational messaging of the sacred and divine LOGOS was totally distinct from the irrational occult gibberish of the Ephesian grammata. Now 'logos', as indicated in *The Elijah Tapestry*, had some unfortunate nuances. It was a mystical term that referred to the golden ratio and was considered in Platonic philosophy and Pythagorean theurgy to be Manifest Deity in mathematical form. John swept these notions aside with a simple expedient: he began his gospel with a number the Pythagoreans regarded as 'abominable' and made his opening sentence 17 words long. That alone would have been enough for his readers to realise the Logos he was referring to was not Gnostic, nor Platonic, nor Pythagorean.

John's balancing act was exquisitely fine. On the one hand, he has avoided the use of 'grammata' for *word*; on the other, he has decried any abstraction of the Logos to a logical, mathematical theory and insisted that the Logos is a 'he', a material flesh-and-blood being, totally human yet also wondrously divine. He was, and is, Immanuel—*God with us.*

1.5 John and Jonah

John begins his gospel with a sweeping movement down from the heaven of heavens into the Day of God's Name. He invites us briefly into the courts of the Logos, where the source of life rules—illumined by sevenfold light. Then he takes us to a baptismal pool on a tributary of the Jordan at the edge of the eastern wilderness.

John's earliest readers might have been distracted by the mention of the *logos* and might momentarily have thought he was welcoming us into that rarefied realm of pure abstracted ideal forms envisaged by Plato. But John rapidly makes clear that the Logos is a living, breathing flesh-and-blood material being. He is not an intangible mathematical blueprint. Nor is He a lifeless word with no purpose other than to facilitate communication.

He is God tabernacled in flesh. He has a name so we can identify Him when He inserts Himself into the flow of history. John's account descends rapidly from timeless eternity to a specific day, a specific location and a specific man. And it is so appropriate that the date he opens with is the Day of God's Name—Yom Kippur, the Day of Atonement. The place is Bethany-beyond-the-Jordan and the man is John the Baptiser, the herald of the Messiah.

Yom Kippur was called 'the Day of God's Name' because it was the only day in the year when God's name could be spoken—and then only by the high priest inside the cloister of the Holy of Holies within the sanctuary of the Inner Court of the Temple.[20] On all other occasions, God was referred to as HaShem, *the Name*.

So it was fitting that, on the Day of God's Name, the Day of Atonement, the Day on which the Jubilee should have been announced,[21] questions of identity became prominent. The leaders in Jerusalem sent messengers out to John the Baptiser to ask him who he claimed to be. As he stood by the baptismal waters, he was peppered with questions about himself. In the parallel section in the last chapter of the gospel, the chiastic mirror, Simon son of Jonah—or John—is likewise quizzed by Jesus.

As noted previously in this series, John the apostle never identifies the mother of Jesus by name. Neither does he identify himself by name. But he uses chiastic parallels to ensure his readers know who he's talking about: the mother of Jesus is mirrored by Mary the Magdalene; the beloved disciple is mirrored by John the Baptiser; Nathanael is mirrored by Thomas—thereby identifying Nathanael as Bartholomew, *son of Tolmai*—Tolmai being the root of the name Thomas.

The name John is said to derive from Hebrew 'Yehochanan', *the Lord is gracious* or *gift of God*. It's one of the most common names in the world.[22] For centuries in western societies it's been the favourite choice of mothers and fathers for their sons, with an

---

[20] Apparently the name spoken was Yahweh which, despite its dominance in the Hebrew Scriptures, is not the identity revealed to Moses at the burning bush. Yahweh means *He is who He is*, and is simply a step closer than HaShem is to God's revealed identity: Ehyeh, *I AM WHO I AM, I will be who I will be*.

[21] Using Christian Gedge's analysis, as detailed in the previous book in this series, *The Summoning of Time: John 2 and 20*.

almost bewildering array of variants.²³ It might seem unlikely that the longstanding meaning could be wrong. But I'm not entirely sure *gift of God* is all there is to say about it.

At the end of John's gospel it's unclear whether Jesus calls Peter 'Simon son of John' or 'Simon son of Jonah'. So there's obviously a strong possibility that John is related to Jonah, *dove*. In addition, there's been a traditional relationship between John and Jonathan—a name with the word for *sea monster* embedded in it.²⁴ The story of Jonah doesn't have anything to do with *doves*,²⁵ but the most famous aspect of it is a *monstrous fish*.

Now up to this point in the gospel narrative, there have been some important interludes involving water:

- John the Baptiser's entire ministry revolved around water and repentance

- Jesus opens His ministry with a sign involving water at a wedding in Cana

Moreover, by the end of the third chapter, we're going to be back with John the Baptiser as he's posed questions about baptism.

---

22   It is the twelfth most common at the time of writing. The most common is said to be Maria, followed by Nushi and then Mohammed. However if the variant spellings of Mohammed—Muhammed, Mohamed and Mohammad—are considered, then it is by far the most popular. See: forebears.io/earth/forenames (accessed 25 March 2024)

23   See, for example, behindthename.com/name/john (accessed 25 March 2024)

24   They are unrelated, etymologically speaking. But in the spiritual world, poetry is supreme when it comes to names and common usage not far behind. The element '-than' in Jonathan means *sea monster*. Similarly Leviathan means *joined sea monster* or perhaps *jointed sea monster*.

25   Surprising since names are carriers of destiny and identity, so some aspect of a dove should appear in his story, however tangential or symbolic. Unless, of course, *dove* is not correct as the meaning.

In the next chapter Jesus will talk to a Samaritan woman about 'living water'. More than half the references to water in the entire New Testament occur in John's gospel plus the Book of Revelation. In my opinion that's because the name John, which in many languages drops the initial J, got entangled in a net with Oannes,[26] the amphibious hybrid man-fish of Mesopotamian mythology. Such dark-light spiritual enmeshing is common over long periods of time.

The monstrous nature of Oannes, a figure depicted in the ruins of Nineveh, *place of fish*, fits well with the overall story of Jonah and his assignment to oppose the spirit of the city. When Jonah pronounced judgment on Nineveh, the Assyrian people responded with repentance. He'd have preferred they remained obdurate and reaped the destruction they'd sown. But they were whole-hearted in fasting and contrition.

The Book of Jonah ends with the words of God:

> *'Should I not have concern for the great city of Nineveh, in which there are more than a hundred and twenty thousand people who cannot tell their right hand from their left—and also many animals?'*

Jonah 4:11^{NIV}

God's question has hung, unanswered, for centuries, awaiting a reply. To pick up the conversation where it left off, a namesake of Jonah would have to appear and take up the unfinished task: the people of Nineveh had repented merely on the basis of the proclamation,

---

26 Originally Uan, the first of seven Apkallu—that is, 'wise' demi-gods sent up from the watery abyss to help mankind. The Babylonians and Assyrians saw these entities as benefactors to humanity, the Hebrews regarded them as malevolent beings responsible for revealing hidden knowledge that encouraged perversion and wickedness.

Yet forty days, and Nineveh shall be overthrown!

Jonah 3:4^{NKJV}

Jonah did not lead them beyond their own instinctive acts of repentance into a knowledge of God and His love and compassion. He did not introduce the people of Nineveh to Yahweh. Had he done so at this point in history, the rise of Assyria would have been completely different—it is likely to have become an ally of Israel, not the superpower that dispersed ten of the twelve tribes out amongst the nations.

Perhaps, in part, Jonah was incensed that the Assyrians repented so promptly while the Israelites were so resistant. It was unbearable to see God have mercy on the enemies of Israel, knowing that without change all his own people could hope for was justice. In his pain, Jonah judged the people of Nineveh as unworthy and God as wrong.

The fourth gospel actually opens by returning to God's unanswered question in the last verse of the Book of Jonah along with the prophet's unfinished assignment. Here we see the conversation pick up again: Jonah's namesake goes out to the people and cries out for repentance.

Jonah's mantle—which, as noted in *The Elijah Tapestry*, was also Elijah's mantle—was passed to John the Baptiser so that he could advance the unfinished tasks of both prophets towards fulfilment. For Jonah, that incomplete assignment was a call for repentance and a proclamation of the kingdom of God. John the Baptiser did what Jonah could not bring himself to do: preach the name of Yahweh and call for a turning back to Him. Jonah could have done this in Nineveh but he went no further than pronouncing the city's doom. Yet, as noted in *The Elijah Tapestry*, if he'd taken the opportunity to teach the Assyrians about God then perhaps the rise of that cruel empire might have been averted.

In retrospect, it was God's intent for Elijah, Elisha and Jonah to spread a knowledge of Himself amongst the Gentiles. However, they all baulked at the prospect. At least in Jonah's case, he didn't want mercy to prevail—and so the pitiless destruction of the Assyrians a century later is exactly what he reaped for his own people. Yet it was not only a war that might have been prevented, it's clearly a war God *wanted* to prevent.

It's the kindness of God to blind us to the long-term havoc resulting from our failure to walk out the calling wrapped in our name.

Now John the apostle, like John the Baptiser, simply couldn't help himself when it came to water. It's so much part of his identity that the mention of it just keeps bubbling up in his writing. And by 'part of his identity', I don't mean because he was a fisherman. I mean that his name, originally dedicated to God, had over many centuries been infiltrated by the myth of the water being, Oannes.[27]

Therefore the new birth—the birth accompanied by water and Spirit and symbolised by baptism with its renunciation of other gods—was as important for John as it was for Nicodemus.

---

[27] Consider also Shaun, Sean and Sion as Celtic variations on John; and the matching Celtic water-god, Shony. Ian and Eoin may derive from Uan, the original form of Oannes.

1.6 Chiasmus

Sometimes called 'introverted parallelism',[28] chiasmus was a literary mirroring technique that was usually applied to letters, words, paragraphs and chapters. The reflective elements could also be ideas.

This quote from Dorothy Sayers is chiastic in nature: 'Work is not, primarily, a thing one does to live, but the thing one lives to do.' In this thought, 'live' and 'do' are reversed in an introverted parallelism.

Jesus used a similar chiastic effect when He said:

>'The Sabbath was made for man
>
>not
>
>man for the Sabbath.'[29]

The words 'Sabbath' and 'man' are the elements that are reversed to produce the chiasmus.

Genesis 9:6[ESV] offers us another simple example:

---

[28] The Scriptural examples in this section are from chiasmusxchange.com/explanatory-notes/ (accessed 4 April 2024) This kind of mirror reflection when applied to mathematics is called palindromes.

[29] Mark 2:27

A		Whoever sheds
	B	the blood
		C of man
		C' by man
	B'	shall his blood
A'		be shed

This literary device was much favoured by the prophets and they employed it in rich and complex ways, sometimes across an entire chapter or more. John has taken chiasmus to a whole new level in his gospel by applying it to the whole book. By splitting his messaging into two parts John has created a symbol of covenant—two divided elements that are one unity—and by continually shifting between the beginning and the end he has created a movement like the 'walk of blood' a person would undertake in accepting a covenant.

As we move back and forward in looking at the verses, may we indeed raise a covenant with Jesus through a union with Him as the Word.

John's messaging can only really be fully understood by looking at both chiastic sections and it is here, in the third chapter and its matching bookend, that this becomes completely apparent. The meaning of the riddling statement, *'Unless you are born again, you cannot see the Kingdom of God,'* [30] is not revealed until the chiastic scene at the Cross at Calvary.

Nicodemus links both these passages, thus preparing us to understand that the Cross was not a death but a birth, not a funeral but a wedding.

---

30   John 3:3[NLT]

Now there was a man of the Pharisees named Nicodemus, a leader of the Jews.

He came to Jesus at night and said, 'Rabbi, we know that You are a teacher who has come from God. For no one could perform the signs You are doing if God were not with Him.'

Jesus replied, 'Truly, truly, I tell you, no one can see the kingdom of God unless he is born again.'

'How can a man be born when he is old?' Nicodemus asked. 'Can he enter his mother's womb a second time to be born?'

John 3:1-4 BSB

Afterward, Joseph of Arimathea, who was a disciple of Jesus
(but secretly for fear of the Jews), asked Pilate to let him
remove the body of Jesus. Pilate gave him permission,
so he came and removed His body.

Nicodemus, who had previously come to Jesus at night,
also brought a mixture of myrrh and aloes,
about seventy-five pounds.

So they took the body of Jesus and wrapped it in linen cloths
with the spices, according to the Jewish burial custom.

Now there was a garden
in the place where Jesus
was crucified, and in the
garden a new tomb in which
no one had yet been laid.

And because it was the Jewish
 day of Preparation
and the tomb was nearby,
they placed Jesus there.

John 19:38–42 BSB

2.1 Man of the Breakthrough

Now there was a man of the Pharisees named Nicodemus, a leader of the Jews. He came to Jesus at night.

John 3:1–2^{BSB}

Nicodemus, who had previously come to Jesus at night, also brought a mixture of myrrh and aloes, about seventy-five pounds.

John 19:39^{BSB}

FIRST CENTURY READERS OF JOHN'S GOSPEL, well-versed in current affairs and recent Jewish history, would probably have done a double-take on encountering the name 'Nicodemus'. Their most likely reaction would have been: surely not *that* Nicodemus! But after that initial surprise, as the evidence piled up—a Pharisee, a leader of the Jews, the mention of Cana a little more than a dozen verses back, the entire conversation revolving around birth and babies—it would quickly have dawned on the readers that Buni ben Gurion, nicknamed Nicodemus, *Man of the Breakthrough*, was exactly the person John was referring to. No doubt whatsoever.

Nicodemus was so famous that most of John's readers would have known about his background. He had legendary status and was mentioned several times in the Talmud.[31] As soon as any reader

---

[31] He is mentioned in Ta'anit 19b, Gittin 56a, Ketubot 65a, 66a, and also Lamentations Rabbah, Ecclesiastes Rabbah as well as *The Jewish War* by Flavius Josephus.

recalled the stories about him, they would have realised that the summoning-of-time theme has not vanished but is still very much present. The 'sign' that Jesus performed at Cana is very much linked to the name 'Nicodemus'.

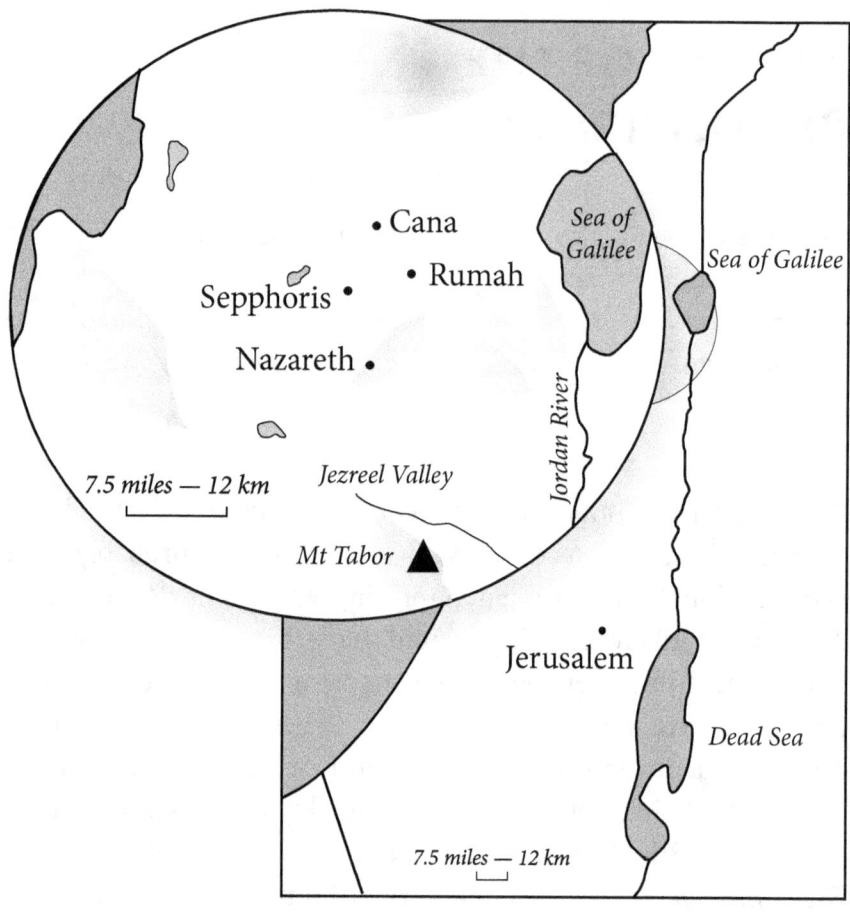

Buni ben Gurion was a very wealthy and highly respected Pharisee. He lived in Jerusalem and had family estates at Rumah in Galilee. Rumah is only about five kilometres[32] from Cana and about twelve[33] from Nazareth. He had a reputation as a righteous

---

32   Three miles.
33   Seven miles.

and generous man who acquired the nickname 'Nicodemus' as the result of a miraculous answer to prayer.

At one time Buni realised that pilgrims to Jerusalem during the festivals had no water to drink. So he went to an official[34] and proposed a deal: in return for access to the water from twelve wells, he would either refill the cisterns by a certain date or else pay twelve hundred talents of silver.[35] It was a stunning amount of money to pledge—and an almost incomprehensible risk.

The day of reckoning came. In the morning, the official sent a message to Buni demanding payment. Buni sent word back that he had until sundown. 'The day is mine,' he said. At noon, the official sent a message to Buni, again demanding payment. Buni sent word back once more that he had until sundown. 'The day is mine,' he repeated.

At sunset, the official and Buni met. Buni was heading for the Temple. The official was going to the public baths. Once again, the official demanded payment. Buni requested leave to pray first. Going into the Temple, he said, 'Creator of the universe, You know that I did not do this for my own glory or for the glory of my father's house. It was for the glory of Your name that I borrowed the water from those wells for the pilgrims in Jerusalem.'

Outside, rain began bucketing down out of the sky. It was such an enormous deluge in such a short time that the twelve wells were filled right up to the brim.

When Buni left the Temple, he once again encountered the official and pointed out that the wells were full and the debt was paid.

---

34 Probably the Roman governor.
35 Valued today at between 30 and 60 million dollars, depending on whether the talents were according to Roman or Hebrew reckoning. Silver varies in price over time and is currently at an historic low. Ten years ago, the values just quoted would have been double the present amount.

However, despite getting all the water back, the official was far from satisfied. He explained the rain came too late. The day was over, it was past sunset and so, strictly speaking, the water had not been returned by the due date. Under the letter of the law the money was still owed. He insisted Buni pay up.

Buni requested just a few minutes to pray again. He returned to the Temple and his prayer, this time, was utterly audacious. 'Creator of the Universe,' he implored, 'show the world that You have favourites.'

Then he went back outside.

And the sun was shining in the sky and the day was just about to finish. The official said, 'Had the sun not broken through, I would have had a claim on you.'[36]

Because of the official's words that the sun had broken through, Buni was ever after known as Naqdimon, *Man of the Breakthrough*,[37] or as Nicodemus, *victory for the people*.[38]

According to the Jewish sages, he was one of only three people for whom time was altered. They suggest that the other two were Joshua and Moses,[39] though to my mind, the pair would be Joshua and Hezekiah.[40]

---

36   This story is told in the Talmud: Taanit 19b:1. In Hebrew calendar reckoning, the day ends at sunset.
37   'Naqdimon' is Hebrew.
38   Nicodemus is Greek and has a different meaning to Naqdimon. The Greek word includes the name of the goddess of victory, Nike, who was worshipped at the Acropolis in Athens in combination with Athena. As noted in *The Summoning of Time: John 2 and 20*, Athena is the Greek face of the Canaanite war goddess, Anat, and her Egyptian counterpart Neith. Thus the name Nicodemus links back to the Cana story both in its references to appointed time, to alterations in the flow of time and to a battle goddess.

However, as noted in the previous volume, the 'sign' at Cana was essentially a dilation of time. Water turns to wine each day along grape vines; but it takes a season, not seconds.

---

39   Joshua of course is easy to understand. It would be at the battle on the Ascent of Beth-Horon, when he asked the sun and moon to stand still. However, I have not been able to discover what incident the sages are thinking about when they nominate Moses as the second person.

40   Isaiah might be more appropriate than Hezekiah, since it was Isaiah who asked Hezekiah what 'sign' he'd like to indicate he would recover—the shadow of the sun moving forward on a sundial-stair or moving backward.

2.2 Wordplay

THERE MUST HAVE BEEN A TWINKLE in the eye of Jesus all the way through His night-time conversation with Buni. There are jokes and puns flying, some of them based on the name Buni and some of them prophetically foreshadowing Buni's acquisition of the title, *Man of the Breakthrough*. Jesus was having a lot of fun. If Buni had been hiding his identity in that afterhours visit, Jesus was letting him know—at every opportunity—that it wasn't working.

First of all, there's the name Buni itself. It might come from 'banah', to *build* or *have children* or it might come from 'binah', *understanding*.

> *Are you the teacher of Israel and yet you do not understand these things?*
>
> John 3:10[ESV]

Here Jesus builds a pun on that possible meaning, *understanding*. His dialogue deliberately plays with the idea of having children, focussing in on the second aspect of Buni's name—ben Gurion. The name Gurion means *whelp*, and usually refers to *a young lion*. However, it can be metaphorically applied to any kind of infant.

Thus Buni ben Gurion could mean *builder, son of young lion* or *understanding, son of baby*.[41] Jesus was forcing Nicodemus into an intellectual wrestle with his identity and thus, ultimately, with his calling. And this was at a time when he wasn't yet called Nicodemus: that nickname was still to come.

In addition, Jesus puns about *miracles* when He talks of being *lifted up*—since the Hebrew word for *miracle*, 'nes', is related to the word for *sign* and *lifted up*. John pivots on the words of Jesus, directing our attention back and forward through time. When he records the statement, 'the Son of Man must be lifted up,' he's reminding us of the miracle in the time of Moses when a bronze snake was raised on a pole for the healing of the people. Yet he's looking forward to the miracle of salvation that Jesus will bring by being lifted up on the Cross. Then he's also pointing us on past that moment towards Buni's own future—that stupendous miracle on behalf of the people.

Both piercing and water are critical elements at the crucifixion—heralding, as we shall see, the new birth, the birth from above. Piercing and water are also critical elements in the emergence (can we think *birth?*) of Nicodemus from Buni. He is known as the *Man of the Breakthrough* after he prays for water and for time. The title comes from the rueful words of the official, 'Had the sun not *broken* through, I would have had a claim on you.' However, that first phrase can also be rendered, 'Had the sun not *pierced* through, I would have had a claim on you.'

By merely mentioning the name Nicodemus, John not only alludes to time factors, linking back to the miracle of Cana, that first of seven signs given by Jesus, but also to the piercing of the Sun of Righteousness for the rebirth of the world.

---

41 See: randomgroovybiblefacts.com/the_pharisee_who_followed.html (accessed 23 August 2024)

The piercing of Jesus' side is unique to John's gospel—none of the other evangelists mention it in connection with the crucifixion. John not only included it, he augmented its significance in several ways so that the reader would be sure to notice it. He drew attention to it by the parallel with the story of Nicodemus, a man famed for a breakthrough piercing of light and time. And if the reader missed that, then there's another clue. Immediately after the description of the piercing of Jesus', John twice swears to the truth of his testimony.[42] The emphasis shows how central the breakthrough, the piercing, was in John's thinking. He wants to ensure we've got the message, one way or another.

---

42   John makes much of his eyewitness status. This is particularly true when it comes to the crucifixion and resurrection. A significant reason for this would have been to counter the claims of Cerinthus and the Gnostics. John was attempting to undermine any validity of their interpretation about the events at the Cross by simply implying they hadn't been there. He anticipated the counter-argument that neither had the other gospel writers and side-stepped it. His account is the only record to have been written by someone who was actually present at the crucifixion. It is important for him therefore, given the teaching of the Gnostics that the 'Christ' was a spirit who had separated from the material flesh of Jesus just prior to the Cross, to make the point and reiterate it that this was a first-hand testimony.

2.3 A Visitor by Night

Nicodemus is sometimes described by preachers as 'sneaky' or 'cowardly' because he came to Jesus secretly, under cover of darkness. Not in the light of day. That, however, is to miss the point—at least in my view.

He was a member of the Sanhedrin, the ruling elite of the Jewish people. He was immensely wealthy and he was generous to a fault. To approach Jesus openly was to risk endorsing a false Messiah. Better to come quietly and check Him out, to make sure of His credentials, to get a feel for His integrity when He's away from the public eye.

It's clear that the conversation between Jesus and Nicodemus isn't an exercise in entrapment. It's more like a dialogue between a rabbi and his student. The whole tenor of Nicodemus' approach is that of courtesy and honour. Jesus opens with some enigmatic statements and Nicodemus strives his best to unravel their meaning. He submits to the authority of Jesus, just as a respectful pupil would to a revered teacher.

But ultimately he doesn't get answers to his questions. That's because they aren't available yet. They are only revealed in the chiastic episode when Nicodemus is at the Cross.

That scene also, by the way, is one of monumental darkness. Luke described it this way:

> *It was now about noon, and darkness came over the whole land until three in the afternoon, for the sun stopped shining.*
>
> Luke 23:45^{NIV}

The meetings of Jesus and Nicodemus are either at night or during the peculiar eclipse that occurred during the crucifixion. That's the specific word Luke uses—'eclipse'—for those English translations that say *the sun stopped shining* or *its light failed* or *it was darkened.*

Now perhaps he didn't mean 'eclipse' in a technical sense but, if so, it seems strange that he didn't use *cloud-covered* or *dust-shrouded* or *smoke-obscured* if that's what he really meant. Instead he uses a word with preternatural overtones. Preternatural, because a solar eclipse lasts just a few minutes, not hours. Besides, it was Passover and thus the day of a full moon. Therefore the configuration of the sun and moon was in exactly the opposite alignment needed for a solar eclipse to occur. Granted, the placements would have been perfect for a lunar eclipse—however, lunar eclipses never happen during the daytime, only at night. And once again, there's no total blackout except for a short period.

Something was most definitely unnatural about positions of the sun and the moon if Luke used accurate terminology in stating this was an eclipse. And since the sun and the moon were the measures of time in those days, time was completely out of joint.

Once again, we're reminded of that first sign at Cana where Jesus summoned Time to change water into wine in minutes instead of months. And we're reminded of time turning back, of water filling twelve wells, and of the sun breaking through for the Man of the Breakthrough.

2.4 Visitors from the East

> *'Nicodemus... also brought a mixture of myrrh and aloes, about seventy-five pounds.'*
>
> John 19:39[BSB]

This is the second time myrrh is mentioned in the gospels. Oils and ointments scented with myrrh are mentioned several times but there is only one other time that *pure myrrh*, 'smurna', is recorded. That happens at the beginning of Matthew's gospel. As a consequence, the tetralogy by the four evangelists is bookended, almost chiastically, with a significant mention of this precious resin:

> *Behold, the star which they had seen in the East went before them, till it came and stood over where the young Child was. When they saw the star, they rejoiced with exceedingly great joy. And when they had come into the house, they saw the young Child with Mary His mother, and fell down and worshipped Him. And when they had opened their treasures, they presented gifts to Him: gold, frankincense, and myrrh.*
>
> Matthew 2:9–11[NKJV]

Here Matthew presents the visit of the magi—traditionally the 'wise men' from the East. Matthew uses the very specific term 'magi', indicating they belonged to the centuries-old patrician class who were the power-brokers and scholarly elite of Babylon.

By the time John set down his own testimony of the life of Jesus, the other gospels had probably been circulating for decades and their contents would have been well-known amongst informed believers. In fact, on many occasions, to capture the fullness of John's narration of events it's necessary to be acquainted with the contents of the other gospels. As we've seen previously in this series, John never names the mother of Jesus—yet the extraordinary revelations involving Mary the Magdalene hidden within his chiastic structure heavily depend on the reader knowing that the Lord's mother was also named Mary.[43]

Now John obviously mentioned 'smurna', *pure myrrh*, in relation to Nicodemus in order to evoke the birth narrative of Jesus and create a link between the first and final appearances of Nicodemus. The mention of 'smurna', only previously specified in relation to Jesus as a baby, is a deliberate reminder of that night-time conversation about the new birth. In fact, John is trying to tell us through this connection that Jesus' death also entailed a birth. To bolster that explanation, he's paralleled myrrh-bringing Nicodemus with the myrrh-bringing magi.

A nifty correlation. But is this all it is? Is this merely a simple and superficial case of two separate parties bringing the same aromatic

---

43 John even relies on his readers having access to common knowledge. Nathanael is never identified as Bartholomew in any gospel—it can only be deduced from systematic elimination. Yet the chiastic scenes that match Nathanael and Thomas make much more sense if Bartholomew and Thomas are paralleled, since both Bartholomew and Thomas have a common linguistic source in the name Tolmai. See Anne Hamilton, *The Summoning of Time: John 2 and 20*, Armour Books 2024

resin in honour of a birth? (Even if one of those births looked like a death.) Or is John giving us a clue about Nicodemus? After all, both the magi and Nicodemus:

- brought myrrh
- intended their visits to Jesus to be secret
- were exceedingly wealthy aristocrats
- were intellectuals of the ruling class

The magi of Babylon were the first to determine the cycle of eclipses and to predict when and where they would appear on the earth's surface. We still use their term for such cycles: 'saros'. We also still use their time and geometry system. If it seems strange to divide a circle into 360° and each degree into 60 minutes and each angular minute into 60 seconds, it's because we have inherited this ancient way of reckoning measurement from the magi of Babylon.

Now the prophet Daniel had twice been appointed the chief of the magi—advisers skilled in astronomy and astrology, mathematics and geometry, dream interpretation, understanding natural phenomena.[44] Pythagoras, the famous Greek mathematician, studied with them—not voluntarily, at least in the first instance—since he was taken to Babylon after being captured in Egypt by invading Persian armies. Pythagoras apparently missed meeting Daniel—who'd been whisked off further east—by just a few years.

Given the deep inroads of Pythagorean Gnosticism into Christianity, and given the statements of early second century church leaders that John wrote his gospel to counter those effects, it is possible—perhaps even likely—that Nicodemus has been set up as an opposing figure, not so much to the magi, as to Pythagoras.

---

44   See: worldhistory.org/Magi/ (accessed 2 November 2023)

The actions of Nicodemus immediately after the death of Jesus make it clear that he had extraordinary faith the resurrection would occur—and that it would also entail new birth as well as a marriage.

In his belief of the reunion of body and soul, Nicodemus was a complete contrast to the Gnostics who believed in reincarnation—the soul transmigrating to a completely new body. In fact, members of the Pythagorean Brotherhood amongst the Gnostics considered that Jesus was the reincarnation of their illustrious founder.

So Nicodemus, for John, may be the ideal representative of the magi and, in addition, his counterpoint for the revered sage, Pythagoras of Samos.

2.5 The Mountain of Spices

75 POUNDS. 34 KILOGRAMS. 100 *litra*.

One hundred litra is the measure of the myrrh and aloes reported by John. Nicodemus together with Joseph of Arimathea wrapped the body of Jesus with the resins and spices and placed it in a new-cut tomb.

Six days previously, Mary of Bethany had broken open an alabaster jar of perfumed ointment:

> *Mary, having taken a litra of fragrant oil of pure nard, of great price, anointed the feet of Jesus and wiped His feet with her hair; and the house was filled with the fragrance of the oil.*
>
> John 12:3[BLB]

In this instance, the descriptor 'pure' for the spikenard must simply mean 'genuine' since the fragrance of the oil filling the house is said to be 'myron' or a *blend of myrrh*. Nard was exceptionally costly because it came along the trade routes from Nepal and was distilled from the rhizomes of an aromatic flowering plant growing high in the Himalayas.

Mary used one litra of anointing mixture; Nicodemus used one hundred litra. If her gesture was extravagant, how much more so was his? If her gesture was wasteful, how much more so was his? If her gesture was irresponsible, how much more so was his? Compared to her solitary jar, he brings in a veritable mountain of myrrh and aloes. Was he aware he was fulfilling the prophecy of the coming of the Bridegroom in the very last verse of the Song of Songs?

> *Make haste, my beloved, and be like a gazelle or a young stag on the mountains of spices.*
>
> Song of Songs 8:14^{ESV}

These are the words of the Bride as she waits for her beloved to cross over the mountain of spices. The word translated *stag* would more appropriately be rendered *strong leader* or *foremost captain*. The verse expresses the Bride's longing for the Bridegroom. Its fulfilment in the tomb of Jesus where the mountain of spices was made manifest is a divine affirmation of the betrothal of the Lamb.

The two most prominent discussion points in the third chapter of John's gospel are the new birth and the Bridegroom. The new birth is the topic in the conversation between Jesus and Nicodemus, and the Bridegroom is the topic when John the Baptiser talks to his disciples about the ministry of Jesus.

These two themes have their culmination during the crucifixion and its aftermath. It might be a death, but it's also a birth and a wedding. Nicodemus in fact steps into the role of the Friend of the Bridegroom vacated at the death of John the Baptiser. He does so by supplying the traditional 'oil of joy' for the wedding: myrrh.

However he's not the only one at the tomb. Apart from the women, Nicodemus is helped in preparing Jesus' body for burial by Joseph of Arimathea. The name Joseph, as is indicated in *The Summoning of Time*, is a major chiastic clue that Jesus is in the process of dealing with grave generational problems that go back to the time when the patriarch Joseph was in Egypt. This includes dispossession of the Egyptians, allowing them no avenue to recover their inheritance after the famine. It also includes the concept of forced resettlement by government.

Perhaps Arimathea provides us with another clue. It was originally Ramathaim-zophim, the birthplace of the prophet Samuel.

2.6 The New Samuel

> *Joseph of Arimathea, who was a disciple of Jesus (but secretly for fear of the Jews), asked Pilate to let him remove the body of Jesus. Pilate gave him permission, so he came and removed His body.*
>
> John 19:38[BSB]

IN THE FIRST VOLUME IN THIS SERIES, *The Elijah Tapestry*, we've seen that Jesus was specifically identified in John's chiastic first and last chapters as:

- the Word
- the Light
- the Life
- Immanuel
- the Christ
- the new Moses
- the new Jacob
- the new Israel
- the new Joshua
- the new Phinehas

- the war messiah known as the 'Son of Joseph'
- the priestly messiah like Melchizedek
- the Elijah-who-is-to-come
- the Son of Man
- the Son of God.

In the second volume in this series, *The Summoning of Time*, we've seen that John reinforced many of those identifications, but also added in additional ones:

- the new Noah
- the new Joseph
- the new Adam.

Many of these will again be reinforced in the third and third-last chapter, and yet another identification will subtly be added in:

- the new Samuel.

Now, the first question I ask myself when an identification like this emerges is: why is a new Samuel needed? How did Samuel fail to fulfil his calling?

I came to realise how important this question was when I was writing *The Summoning of Time*. The sudden realisation that the pair of chiastic quotes from the saga of Joseph of Egypt pointed to something terribly wrong in the life of someone I'd always thought of as an unalloyed hero—apart, of course, from a fair bit of brattish behaviour in his teenage years—was a real wake-up call. Ever since that time, when I'm asked to pray with someone about dispossession that involves the government, I ask them to speak out forgiveness to Joseph for his part in creating systemic disinheritance. The results have been, on occasion, so swift and spectacular, everyone involved with the prayer has been surprised.

It's not difficult to see parallels in the life of Jesus and Samuel. In fact Hannah, the mother of Samuel, is the first person in the Scriptural record to proclaim that the Lord has a Messiah and moreover that the Messiah is a king.[45] This prophecy occurs at the finale of her song of praise:

> *The Lord judges the ends of the earth. He gives strength to His King and lifts the head of His Messiah.*
>
> 1 Samuel 2:10[GWT]

Her canticle of rejoicing over the birth of her son is the basis of the Magnificat—Mary's paean of praise to God when she is expecting Jesus. Her response to the Spirit-inspired greeting of her cousin Elizabeth immediately evokes the exultant song of Hannah in gratitude to God for blessing her with Samuel:

My heart rejoices in the Lord; my horn is exalted in the Lord… because I rejoice in Your salvation.	*My soul magnifies the Lord, and my spirit rejoices in God my Saviour.*
1 Samuel 2:1[NASB]	Luke 1:46–47[ESV]

Samuel was a miracle child, as was Jesus. Samuel's parents were devout and God-fearing. They visited the Tabernacle at Shiloh regularly, and made a sacrifice for the dedication of Samuel to the Lord's service. Likewise, both Mary and Joseph were devout and God-fearing. They attended the Temple and offered a sacrifice for the dedication of Jesus as an infant. The incident where they

---

45 She is credited with inventing the action of rocking in prayer, still often seen practised by observant Jews. She is also the first to call on God by the name Yahweh Sabaoth, the Lord of Hosts, the Commander of Angel Armies. See: Anne Hamilton and Natalie Tensen, *As Resplendent as Rubies: The Mother's Blessing and God's Favour Towards Women II*, Armour Books 2020.

found Him in the Temple when He was twelve suggests they went regularly to observe the Feasts.

The boy Samuel continued to grow in stature and in favour with the Lord and with people.	*Jesus grew in wisdom and stature, and in favour with God and man.*
1 Samuel 2:26^{NIV}	Luke 2:52^{NIV}

Samuel established the kingship in Israel by anointing Saul and then later David. Jesus established the kingship of the Son of David.

Samuel was the last judge of Israel. Before he was born, the priests at the Tabernacle were so corrupt that God decreed a curse on the house of Eli, the high priest. Eli's sons sexually abused the women serving at the Tabernacle, and also instructed their aides to physically abuse worshippers in order to get the best of the offerings. They defiled the sanctuary with their blasphemy and dishonest dealings. Eli criticised his sons but did nothing to stop them.

No doubt the Israelites were crying out to God for a deliverer. And, because His answer was Samuel, their prayers would have been ascending for decades. Samuel had to be born, be dedicated to Temple service, grow up and learn all about ministering to the Lord so that when Eli and his sons died—all on the same day—and the Ark of the Covenant was captured by the Philistines, he would be ready to take over. How old was Samuel when that happened? We don't know—but, to be recognised by the people as the successor of Eli, he would probably have been thirty. Yes, around the same age as Jesus when He began His ministry.

Up until that time, with the notable exception of the occasion the Lord spoke to him as a child in the Tabernacle, silence surrounds

Samuel's upbringing. The same is true for Jesus. With the notable exception of the time He was found in the Temple, expounding to the elders there, silence surrounds His upbringing.

Samuel was, according to Peter in Acts 3:24, the first of the prophets. Peter isn't entirely ignoring the likes of Moses or Deborah who preceded Samuel—he apparently meant Samuel was the first to be *the head of a school of prophets*. Just as Jesus was the Head of a school of disciples.

Samuel was a high priest—but not of the lineage of Aaron.[46] Jesus too is our High Priest—again not of the lineage of Aaron. Instead Jesus has been appointed according to the order of Melchizedek.

Samuel was a Nazarite. Jesus was a Nazarene. This comparison might seem a bit suspect. However there's a very real problem with the verse describing Joseph's decision to move to Nazareth after he brings Mary and Jesus back from Egypt:

> *So the family went and lived in a town called Nazareth. This fulfilled what the prophets had said: 'He will be called a Nazarene.'*
>
> Matthew 2:23[NLT]

There's no known Scripture that Matthew is quoting. Various artful dodges have been proposed to resolve the dilemma, none of them to my mind especially convincing. The simplest solution is that

---

[46] The books of Samuel give the impression he came from the tribe of Ephraim and never mention any Levite heritage. 1 Chronicles 6:22-27, however, details Samuel's descent from Levi, but not through Aaron. Strictly Samuel was not entitled to be a priest, let alone high priest. God apparently made an exception for him because of the corruption of the sons of Eli and the need for a replacement of their entire line once it had come under a divine curse. God had decreed there could be no atonement for the blasphemy of the sons so their sacrifices on their own behalf and that of others would be ineffective.

these words are based on the prophetic statement of the angel to the wife of Manoah in Judges 13:5 that Samson is to be a Nazarite.

Now a Nazarite—someone who makes a vow, usually temporary, to abstain from wine and even grapes, who doesn't cut his hair and doesn't touch a dead body—is not the same as a Nazarene, a resident of Nazareth. Clearly, however, if the match is correct, then poetry is more important to Matthew than any theological precision or exact science involving etymology, semantics or philology.[47]

I don't find this a surprise. Our civilisation has toppled poetry from its once-supreme height. Yet poetic forms are significant in prophecy, in proclamations about the destinies of peoples and towns, in name covenants, and in the design of Scripture. So to overlook them is similar to seeking accurate lyrics while ignoring the evidence of an orchestral symphony.

Now I may not have convinced you that poetry is the answer to the problem. However, some of the other possible resolutions to this dilemma rely on poetry too, but much more tenuously.

So back to the question, what did Samuel do wrong? Why did there have to be a new Samuel? Samuel failed to parent well. His

---

[47] There's always the possibility, of course, that Matthew was being literal, not poetical. It may perhaps be that the residents of Nazareth were actually connected to a Nazarite community. If this is indeed the case, it was probably through the famously teetotal clan of Rechabites who were considered to keep Nazarite-like vows. There is a dispute over whether the Rechabites were counted amongst the Israelites or were non-Israelites. Some commentators consider they were a school of prophets started by Elijah and Elisha, while others regard them as descendants of Moses' father-in-law, Jethro. Regardless, the Rechabites were said to have married their daughters into the tribe of Levi. Early church history contains hints that one of Jesus' brothers was a Rechabite, thereby suggesting that Joseph was and all his siblings were. An examination of the potential links between the Rechabites and the family of Jesus will be left for a later volume in this series.

sons did not grow up to become God-fearing. Instead of taking their father as a role model, they followed in the footsteps of the sons of Eli. They were corrupt, crooked and abusive.

The people, not unnaturally, had no desire to return to the perversions that had been common in the Tabernacle during the days of Eli. So they demanded a king. God pointed out to Samuel that the people hadn't really rejected Samuel, so much as they had rejected the Lord Himself. Nevertheless, the precipitating cause for this unrest was the behaviour of Samuel's sons.

The mission of Jesus included a reversal of this rupture in relationship between God and His people, as well as within society itself. Like John, He preached a gospel of repentance—the Good News was that, in turning back to God and acknowledging Him as both Saviour and King, the year of the Lord's favour would usher in the Kingdom of Heaven.

We can see the turnaround as a result of this historical mending that Jesus accomplished. Samuel's family didn't follow him into national leadership, but the family of Jesus did indeed follow Him into spiritual leadership while also achieving national prominence and contributing to the pastoral epistles disseminated throughout the churches. Certainly there were some decidedly rocky moments of doubt, denial and double-mindedness at times, but nevertheless James—the Lord's brother—as well as Simon Peter, Jesus' impetuous follower, both stepped up to assume significant mantles and to exercise vital roles in the fledgling Christian movement.

The last time Samuel appeared in Scripture was as a ghost. King Saul, facing a massive coalition of Philistine forces, was desperate for divine guidance. Heaven was silent. In despair, Saul sought to consult his deceased mentor Samuel. He engaged the help of a medium from Endor to raise Samuel's spirit from Sheol. In doing so, he covenanted with hell, creating an agreement that still stood in Jesus' day.

Jesus showed His ability to annul Saul's covenant at Nain when He raised the son of a widow from the dead. It's no coincidence that this happens at Nain, which is a neighbouring village to Endor. Nor is it a coincidence that, when Jesus journeyed to raise Lazarus from the dead, He followed the path taken by Saul's bones when they were removed from Gilead and reinterred near Jerusalem.

Jesus didn't make covenants with Death or with Sheol to release their captives. He broke the power of the grave, showing that it was God's plan for bodies as well as spirits to return from the dead and experience fullness of life, blessing upon blessing, wondrous and unstinting favour from the highest heaven.

2.7 'According to Jewish Burial Custom'

Let me do a complete about-face. In the last section we looked at the possible primacy of poetry in relation to solving a quotation problem regarding Matthew's statement about Jesus being prophesied to be a Nazarene. Instead of strict and rigorous accuracy, I suggested we should go with the flow and choose the evoked nuance rather than the exact wording.

But now I want to be pedantic. I want to be meticulous about what's being said by John and what's not being said.

> So they took the body of Jesus and wrapped it in linen cloths with the spices, according to the Jewish burial custom.
>
> John 19:40[BSB]

The problem with this statement is that it somewhat contradicts what John has said earlier in the scene in front of the tomb of Lazarus. Jesus had just asked for the stone to be removed and Martha was horrified. 'Lord, by now he stinks,' she said.[48]

Clearly there were no spices at Bethany. Martha expected a stench. That tells us she'd had at least passing acquaintance with the decay of dead bodies previously. It also tells us that a lack of spices wasn't

---

48 John 11:39[BSB]

unusual. Lazarus hadn't therefore been dishonoured in death by a failure to provide his body with a sweet-smelling aroma.[49]

Arie Uittenbogaard points out that the story of Lazarus gives the reader a swift education in Jewish burial customs. There was no embalming or preserving, common amongst the Egyptians. Instead the body was carefully wrapped in linen—this was to avoid touching it, since if someone did, they would have to isolate for seven days. It was normal to honour the deceased by laying the wrapped body in a tomb by sundown of the same day.

So the wrapping of the body of Jesus was common practice but the provision of spices was not. The aromatic oils, however, did serve a purpose—it warned people to keep their distance. It was a call for privacy. But not because of death. Because of the consummation of a marriage. Myrrh was called 'oil of joy' and was specifically used on the wedding night.

Uittenbogaard comments:

> 'With his hundred *litre*[50] of myrrh-oil (and a hundred is two times fifty, or a double witness to jubilee), Nicodemus unmistakably declared that the marriage of God and mankind had been consummated. He never went there to bury Christ; he went there to see him be "born again," just as Jesus had explained him when the whole Nicodemus

---

49 His sister Mary could, after all, have provided aromatic oils for Lazarus, since she still had the alabaster jar later when she anointed Jesus.

50 Uittenbogaard comments: 'Mary's *litre* represented 300 *dinari*, which was a common man's annual wage. Nicodemus brings one hundred times as much; that's one hundred years of labor worth of myrrh oil. Moving that kind of oil must have involved every merchant in town. There's no way that Nicodemus could have amassed that much oil covertly, or even keep its purpose secret. Surely the whole town knew about it.' See: abarim-publications.com/Meaning/Nicodemus.html (accessed 4 November 2023)

cycle started. The only other time that word σμυρνα (*smurna*) occurs in the gospels is in the nativity story, when the magi from the east gave it to Mary and Jesus when he was born the first time.

'The older gospels had told the story of Christ's burial in Joseph's tomb but none of them mentioned Nicodemus' massive myrrh contribution (in Mark and Luke, the women bring spices; no myrrh is mentioned). It may have occurred to John that the audience of the older three gospels hadn't understood the resurrection as described by the earlier versions, and he may have inserted Nicodemus' outrageous gesture as a kind of inside joke. To people in the know, he couldn't have done it more obviously. A hundred *litre* of myrrh-oil. Custom of the Jews. A garden with a new tomb in which no one had yet laid, which is obvious to anyone a direct reference to the locked garden (the virgin bride) of the Song of Solomon 4:12 and the wafting spices of 4:16 (also see John 3:29).

'All gospels explain that Jesus' Body was placed in the tomb on the day before the Sabbath. And all gospels tell that the women went to the grave the day after Sabbath. Not a single member of a Jewish audience would have assumed that the women went to the tomb to embalm a person who'd been dead for two nights and a day (also see John's hint in John 11:31).'[51]

The wrapping of a body was normal; but the spices and oils were not. It must have been baffling to the disciples when Jesus said at the meal at Bethany after He'd been anointed by Mary, '*Leave her alone. She did this in preparation for my burial.*'[52]

---

51 See: abarim-publications.com/Meaning/Nicodemus.html (accessed 4 November 2023)

52 John 12:7[NLT]

It would have been completely enigmatic to the guests at that dinner. 'Burial?' they'd have thought. 'What's He talking about? This is the aroma of a wedding.'

The new birth and the wedding are inextricably linked. Jesus was swaddled in linen in the tomb just as He was swaddled in the manger. It was a tomb that had never been used before—unusual, since family tombs were re-used over and over across centuries, the bones being gathered up after a few years and bundled with the ancestors. It's a virgin tomb, just as Jesus had once been placed in a virgin womb.

As for the wrappings—there's something of a mystery there. Lazarus had needed someone to unwrap him. But the graveclothes lay in the tomb when Peter and John arrived there as if the resurrected body of Jesus had just passed through them. As later He was to pass through the locked door of the upper room.

Fortunately for Jesus, as Mark's gospel tells us, a young man had lost his clothes in the garden not far from the tomb just a few days previously.[53]

---

53   Mark 14:52

2.8 Symphony of Names

> *Jesus replied, 'Truly, truly, I tell you, no one can see the kingdom of God unless he is born again.'*
> *'How can a man be born when he is old?' Nicodemus asked. 'Can he enter his mother's womb a second time to be born?'*
>
> John 3:3–4[BSB]

THROUGHOUT THE ANCIENT WORLD, names were prophetic indicators of an individual's calling in life—a daily reminder of the destiny prepared for them, a foreshadowing of their divine purpose. Identity today may be increasingly based on race or gender, political persuasion or social class, but in the deep past, it was simply a matter of name.

Some of us today think so little of names that we regard changing them as merely a label swap, a brand refresh, an exterior makeover. But for our ancestors, a different name meant a different destiny, and the *change* indicated an *exchange* had taken place. It wasn't merely a matter of taking on a new name, it meant that you'd traded names with another person in a covenant ceremony involving pledges of friendship between the partners, their families and their descendants.

Such an exchange takes place when God bestows the name Abraham on Abram. He also reveals a new name for Himself in this process: El Shaddai. Similarly, just before Simon receives the new name Peter, the Holy Spirit reveals that Jesus is the Messiah and Simon calls Him that. It's a name exchange: new names or revelations about names for both parties,[54] along with the associated new callings, new vocations, new destiny.

The essence of covenant is not the promises in the contract: it's oneness. In a blood covenant, the partners are bonded into one family—it's no longer *your* family and *my* family, it's *our* family. In a name covenant, the partners are bonded into an unbreakable friendship—it's no longer *you* and *me*, it's *we*.

Now name covenants in Scripture are separated by six days from threshold covenants. In a threshold agreement, the partners become a defensive unity—agreeing to protect each other as if the other is their own self.[55]

John has a distinct focus on name covenants, not just on names. Questions about identity have been ramping up from the start while answers concerning destiny have been forthcoming at the end. As outlined in *The Elijah Tapestry*, the first and last chapters concern the Elijah-who-is-to-come: initially Elijah's mantle

---

54 Name covenants still existed until the early twentieth century. They were used (or, more accurately, abused) by many early European explorers of the Pacific basin, and of Africa, to ensure safe passage in territory where potentially hostile tribes lived. A lingering remnant of the concept is a wife taking her husband's surname, thus uniting his family with hers. See Anne Hamilton, *Name Covenant: Invitation to Friendship*, Armour Books 2018

55 A threshold covenant does not need to be preceded by a name covenant. It can exist in its own right but, if it does, it is usually temporary—for the duration of a guest's visit to a home. In that case, it is simply a rite of hospitality where the host and guest agree to defend each other if the residence is attacked. When, however, a name covenant precedes a threshold covenant by six days, it is a solemn invitation to friendship and, if accepted, has dire ramifications in the case of subsequent betrayal.

was carried by John the Baptiser but later Jesus handed it on to Simon Peter to complete the task left unfinished by Elijah and his successors for nearly nine centuries.

The first chapter ends with the encounter between Jesus and Nathanael—a disciple known only from this mention in John's gospel. By logical deduction, he is elsewhere called Bartholomew and that would be a better choice of name to match up with Thomas, both because Bartholomew and Thomas are names deriving from the same root, Tolmai, and because both men express doubts about Jesus. I'm sure that Nathanael did many more significant things during his time with Jesus than voice a few doubts. So he must be identified here, by this name and no other, for a particular purpose. I suspect that John's choice of name and his choice of story, as a matter of fact, was to present his readers with the first clue pointing to the ancient goddess Anat. *Nath*anael and A*nath*, the common variant spelling for Anat, have syllables in common, and so do N*athana*el and *Athena*, the Greek counterpart of Anat—whose Egyptian equivalent was Neith.

The opening salvo by Jesus in the ongoing war against this spirit of dispossession occurs in Nathanael's hometown of Cana. There He changed water into wine—fine aged wine that was paradoxically new wine, a symbol of returned inheritance. A returned inheritance is, after all, the opposite of dispossession.

The issue of dispossession by Anat goes back, as John makes clear in his quotes from Genesis, to Joseph of Egypt who dispossessed the Egyptians during the famine and gave them no way to buy back the land. He made them slaves in perpetuity. It's no coincidence the name of his wife, Asenath, means *holy to Anat*, or that he himself was called Zaphenath-Paneah by Pharaoh, a name that includes the title *Anat of Zaphon*.

Mary the Magdalene re-enacts part of the ritual search by Anat during the despoiling of Canaanite religion that takes place in the garden after the resurrection. In doing so, she is a participant in the healing of history that goes back to the reign of Athaliah, the daughter of Ahab and Jezebel. Athaliah was the queen who dispossessed the ruling house of Judah and usurped the throne.

Mary's name is also involved in this mending of history. *Mary* and *myrrh* both come from the same root meaning *bitter*, while myrrh's Greek cognate 'smurna' comes from the same root as Samaria, the capital of the kingdom once ruled by Ahab and Jezebel. Samaria, in turn, has a synonym—Magdalene. Both Samaria and Magdalene mean *of the watchtower*.[56] They are also heavily nuanced with overtones of *memorial, memory* and *remembrance*.

As noted in *The Summoning of Time*, I do not believe Mary came from Magdala, but from Bethany.[57] It is my contention that she was given the name 'The Magdalene' by Jesus when He said she would always be remembered for anointing Him with spikenard, smelling of myrrh. Covenants with oil were rare but not unknown. By using myrrh, a substance with a name related to her own, she basically asked Jesus into a covenant involving her own name. And Jesus, in my view, accepted her invitation and gave her a new variant for her name: *rememberer*. That's a pun that transcends the language barrier. It has duality, even in English. *Rememberer* is not just about recalling a memory but about restoring that which is dismembered.

In memory of her, ever after, Mary was dubbed 'Magdalene' for *memorial* or *watchtower*. She was the one who was granted the

---

56   Also meaning *watchtower* is Zaphon in the title, Anat of Zaphon. Zaphon also has other meanings including *north*.

57   The original name of Bethany may have been Anathoth, the hometown of the prophet Jeremiah. Anathoth is named for Anat.

mantle of Joseph of Egypt by Jesus to fulfil the tasks that Joseph had left incomplete—the return of inheritance to the dispossessed, the restoration of the birthrights Anat had dismembered.

Peter was given Elijah's mantle. Mary the Magdalene was given Joseph's mantle.[58] So now, having glanced back at these legacies, we might just begin to suspect that Nicodemus received a very significant mantle too. And of course, he does. This time there's nothing subtle in John's writing about the passing on of the legacy. He's outlined it for us very clearly. Nicodemus, it seems, was given the mantle of Moses—not to repeat the works of the great Teacher and Law-giver, but to finish the tasks that remained unfinished within his calling.

Before we examine those tasks, let's look at Nicodemus' original name. Buni ben Gurion has, as we've seen, more than one possible translation. The word 'gurion' means *young lion*. David Grün, the first Prime Minister of modern Israel, adopted the name David Ben-Gurion on moving from Poland to the Middle East in the first decade of the twentieth century. There are curious overtones to 'gurion': in the spiritual world, there were seventy 'young lions' regarded as the sons of the Canaanite goddess Asherah. They were angelic powers, designated as *principalities*, who ruled over territories, tribal groups and nations. Their leader was Baal-Hadad, their sister was Anat.

Jeremy Chance Springfield points out that 'gurion' arises from 'gur', a *suckling* of either animal or human. He indicates that the name of the father of Nicodemus, therefore, essentially meant a *nursing child* and that Jesus' mention of the need to be born

---

[58] In the garden outside the tomb, she is asked by the 'stranger' she takes for a gardener, 'Who are you looking for?' She therefore stands in the place of Joseph in the re-enactment of the scene where a stranger asks him: 'Who are you looking for?' at the place where his tomb will later be located.

again speaks directly to the family name of Nicodemus. Buni ben Gurion essentially means Buni, *son of an infant*. But how can an infant have a son? What does that mean? It would have to refer to *a child that is not yet born.*[59]

So Jesus, in making the enigmatic statement about being 'born again' was indulging in wordplay and telling Nicodemus that—as his name already spelled out for him—he was not yet born. At least not yet born spiritually. Physically, yes, of water and blood. Yet spiritually, of water and Spirit, no.

Both Nicodemus and John were witnesses to the moment of new birth. They were not alone. Joseph of Arimathea and several women, most of them named Mary, as well as at least one Roman soldier, were in attendance as well. The riddle Jesus posed to Nicodemus was answered at the Cross.

---

59 See: randomgroovybiblefacts.com/the_pharisee_who_followed.html (accessed 22 January 2024)

Jesus answered, 'Truly, truly, I tell you, no one can enter the kingdom of God unless he is born of water and the Spirit. Flesh is born of flesh, but spirit is born of the Spirit. Do not be amazed that I said, "You must be born again." The wind blows where it wishes. You hear its sound, but you do not know where it comes from or where it is going. So it is with everyone born of the Spirit.'

'How can this be?' Nicodemus asked.

'You are Israel's teacher,' said Jesus, 'and you do not understand these things? Truly, truly, I tell you, we speak of what we know, and we testify to what we have seen, and yet you people do not accept our testimony. If I have told you about earthly things and you do not believe, how will you believe if I tell you about heavenly things?

It was the day of Preparation, and the next day was a
High Sabbath. In order that the bodies would not remain
on the cross during the Sabbath, the Jews asked Pilate to
have the legs broken and the bodies removed. So the soldiers
came and broke the legs of the first man who had been
crucified with Jesus, and those of the other.
But when they came to Jesus and saw that
He was already dead, they did not break His legs.
Instead, one of the soldiers pierced
His side with a spear, and i
mmediately blood and water flowed out.
The one who saw it has testified to this,
and his testimony is true.
He knows that he is telling the truth,
so that you also may believe.

John 19:31-35 BSB

Three

3.1 Birth of the Bride

Jesus answered, "Truly, truly, I tell you, no one can enter the kingdom of God unless he is born of water and the Spirit. Flesh is born of flesh, but spirit is born of the Spirit. Do not be amazed that I said, 'You must be born again.'...

'How can this be?' Nicodemus asked.

John 3:5–7;9[BSB]

So the soldiers came and broke the legs of the first man who had been crucified with Jesus, and those of the other.

But when they came to Jesus and saw that He was already dead, they did not break His legs. Instead, one of the soldiers pierced His side with a spear, and immediately blood and water flowed out.

John 19:32–34[BSB]

A QUICK SKIM-READ OF JOHN'S GOSPEL might give us the impression that, unlike the other evangelists Luke and Matthew, there is no nativity scene, no birth narrative, no wonder of angels delivering heavenly messages, no wise and mysterious visitors arriving with costly aromatic gifts. Yet, in fact, two of the major ongoing themes of John's gospel are birth and birthright. In telling the stories about them, John does indeed mention angels and secret, scholarly visitors who eventually bring in a mountain of fragrance.

John definitely does have a birth narrative, but it's not confined to just being born. It's a complex interweaving of several of life's climactic moments. In the previous book in this series, *The Summoning of Time*, the chiastic parallelism between the wedding at Cana and the nuptial allusions at the tomb of Jesus emphasise that John wasn't just writing about death and resurrection but also about birth and marriage. The theme of the Bridegroom building the kingdom for His newborn Bride and then coming for her is threaded all the way through the gospel.

But the birth aspect—the need to be born again, to have been given life by the Spirit as well as by the flesh—was like one of those riddling parables of Jesus. It doesn't make sense unless the Spirit of the Lord Himself interprets it.

Now as Nicodemus stood by the Cross, he'd have seen the soldiers break the legs of the condemned men on either side of Jesus. One of the soldiers then took a lance and pierced His side. Nicodemus would have observed the flow of blood and water.

There must have been a moment, a flesh-raising tingle when his hair stood on end and it dawned on him just what he'd seen. The shudder of the earthquake must have been accompanied by a tremor in his mind and soul as he recalled that long-ago conversation with Jesus about new birth.

He'd just seen a flow of blood and water, after all—the very things that accompany a natural birth. Jesus had told him he had to be born again of water and spirit—but 'spirit' in Greek can also indicate 'blood'.[60] Perhaps, as Nicodemus remembered Jesus' words, his first thought was a rational one. He'd surely have been tempted to dismiss the idea that he was watching the breaking of the waters of birth. It was too ludicrous, too illogical. Instead of birth, he'd seen empirical evidence of death: life had ceased because blood had separated into its constituent elements.

Besides, birth simply doesn't happen through the pierced side of a man.

But Nicodemus was a teacher in Israel. He knew the Torah back to front and inside out. He must have suddenly realised that, in actual fact, such a birth had indeed happened before. It wasn't utterly unique. There was once, *just once,* in the entire history of the world that a similar event had occurred. Eve had been taken from the side of the first man, while he was sleeping. Just as the bride of the First Adam was born from under his heart, so too was the Bride of the Second Adam.

To confirm that this was the perfect day for a wedding, Nicodemus may well have been conscious that the appropriate Scripture to be read at some time after the Passover meal, during the day when Jesus was crucified, was the bridal canticle, Song of Songs.[61] Everything pointed to a wedding and to the birth of the new Eve. And to fulfil the prophecy in the last verse of the Song of Songs, a mountain of spices had to be built.

At some point, the weight of evidence must have felt inescapable. Buni, *builder,* has to have had a breakthrough of *understanding.*

---

60   Not all Greek words for *spirit* can also mean *blood*, but the word, 'haima', used in reference to the blood that flowed from the pierced side of Jesus can indeed do so. 'Haima' can mean: *blood, streams of blood, anything like blood, spirit, courage, bloodshed, murder, blood relationship, kin,* and *kinship*. See: christswords.com/main/content/haima (accessed 8 September 2023) I believe that the reason John chose this particular word with its inbuilt ambiguity of *blood* and *spirit* is because of his target audience. He was making a point to those readers influenced by Gnosticism that their attempt to separate the spirit world from the world of flesh-and-blood—especially their attempts to divide 'Christ' the perfect spirit from 'Jesus' the man—were impossibly wrong.

61   Solomon's Song of Songs, an erotic love poem that has often been interpreted as an allegory of Christ as the Bridegroom of the church, is customarily read on the first night of Passover at the end of the Seder. It thus attains enormous significance in terms of the words of Jesus on the Cross and His subsequent burial.

Yes, he was the Man of the Breakthrough, the man who would later witness a miracle of light piercing the night—but his true breakthrough was long before the day when time reversed after he'd prayed for water to fill twelve dry wells. No wonder he had the faith God would answer his prayer for more time; he'd already expressed incredible and extraordinary faith when he made the decision that myrrh for a wedding was needed when the Second Adam woke from the sleep of death.

The likelihood that Nicodemus had a hundred litra of myrrh on hand on the off-chance the marriage of the Messiah would take place on his watch and in his lifetime is minimal.[62] The very fact he brought so much to the tomb indicates he had come to the stunning realisation he'd witnessed the birth of the Bride of Christ, the new Eve, and that he needed to act on that information.

To be 'born again' meant to enter, by faith, into that wound in the side of Jesus and be brought forth as His child, His Bride, His church. When Nicodemus understood—when he finally came to the *understanding* integral to his name—he didn't stint when it came to a demonstration of his faith that Jesus was sleeping and would soon rise again. Nicodemus sent his servants out, scouring every oil shop in Jerusalem for myrrh and buying it up for the wedding of the Lamb.[63] He'd become, no doubt to his immense surprise, the 'Friend of the Bridegroom' responsible for ensuring the wedding ran smoothly.

---

62 Personally I think the chances are non-existent, but let me err on the conservative side with 'minimal'.
63 In a single afternoon, he has to have bought a million dollars' worth of myrrh at today's rate.

3.2 The Kingdom of God

No one can enter the kingdom of God unless he is born of water and the Spirit.

John 3:5[BSB]

NICODEMUS WAS ONE OF THE RICHEST MEN in first century Judea. Quite apart from his generosity, his wealth marked him out as a man exceptionally blessed by God. More than that, he was revered as a miracle-worker who had prayed to God with intrepid boldness: 'Show the world that You have favourites.'

Now, most rabbinic commentators today interpret God's answer to indicate that the Jewish people were His favourites, not Nicodemus personally. However, back in the first century, it was understood that wealth and nobility were prime indicators of God's favour. Adding in the miracle only confirmed a pre-existing bias within Jewish culture.

John's point in recognising Nicodemus by name, when he all too often obscures the identities of others, would have been a shock to those who still harboured a lingering suspicion that God's favour is evidenced by prosperity and prestige. Jesus had stunned His own disciples by remarking it was hard for the rich to enter the kingdom of heaven:

> 'How hard it will be for those who are wealthy to enter the kingdom of God!'

The disciples were startled by these words, but Jesus told them again,

> 'Children, how hard it is for those who trust in their wealth to get into the kingdom of God! It's easier for a camel to squeeze through the eye of a needle than for a rich person to get into the kingdom of God.'
>
> The disciples were utterly amazed and asked one another, 'Then who can be saved?'

Mark 10:23–26^{ISV}

Jesus' comments were utterly incomprehensible to the disciples who'd been brought up to believe wealth was indicative of merit in God's eyes and therefore likely signified an individual's salvation.

John overturns this thinking, just as Jesus did. By introducing such a famous and respected figure and implying the question, 'If even Nicodemus couldn't get into the Kingdom without being born again, then what possible hope do the rest of us have?', he was trying to produce a seismic shift in the way believers thought about salvation.

If a righteous, generous and wealthy miracle-worker like Nicodemus had no chance of salvation apart from Jesus, then nobody does. John states that clearly but by using Nicodemus as his exemplar, he was able to push the message home in a much deeper way.

3.3 Testimony and Belief

> 'You are Israel's teacher,' said Jesus, 'and you do not understand these things? Truly, truly, I tell you, we speak of what we know, and we testify to what we have seen, and yet you people do not accept our testimony. If I have told you about earthly things and you do not believe, how will you believe if I tell you about heavenly things?'
>
> John 3:10–12[BSB]

> The one who saw it has testified to this, and his testimony is true. He knows that he is telling the truth, so that you also may believe.
>
> John 19:35[BSB]

HERE AT THE BEGINNING OF JOHN'S GOSPEL is the clear declaration of Jesus that the Jewish leaders, the teachers of Israel, have not accepted *'our'* testimony. It's unclear who the *'we'* of *'we speak'*, *'we know'* and *'we testify'* are—some identify *'we'* as the disciples, some as Jesus and His cousin John the Baptiser, some as those who preach the gospel or the kingdom of heaven.

Since John didn't clarify who he meant, perhaps the significance is not so much in the identity of those who were speaking and knowing and testifying as in their plurality. There was more than one of them.

> *Every matter must be established by the testimony of two or three witnesses.*
>
> 2 Corinthians 13:1[NIV]

> *Every matter may be established by the testimony of two or three witnesses.*
>
> Matthew 18:16[BSB]

These statements embody a principle based on one of the statutes of the law of Moses that was designed to minimise the possibility of false accusation:

> *A lone witness is not sufficient to establish any wrongdoing or sin against a man, regardless of what offense he may have committed. A matter must be established by the testimony of two or three witnesses.*
>
> Deuteronomy 19:18[BSB]

According to the wider principle, far more than wrongdoing can be established as a result of the testimony of two or three independent witnesses. Any matter is subject to the same general rule. Therefore the leaders should believe the statements of those who have publicly spoken about their eyewitness experiences, who know first-hand what they've observed and who have testified to the events they've seen and even participated in.

Basically Jesus is asking, 'If you're not going to follow the rule and believe in the testimony of those many witnesses who can verify for you those things that occurred here on earth—water turned into wine, lepers healed, demons cast out, crowds fed with two loaves and five fish—what's the point in speaking of things that occur in heaven?' Now Jesus isn't making a specific allegation against Nicodemus here. When He says 'you', it's a plural 'you', indicating that He's speaking to Nicodemus as a representative of the Pharisees, of the ruling body of the Sanhedrin, and of the Jewish leaders in general.

Right at the end, in the third last chapter, the identity of the one who is testifying to the events surrounding the death of Jesus is likewise unclear. Just as 'we' is ambiguous at the start, so *'the one who saw it'* is also ambiguous. Most scholars think it is the gospel writer himself, and certainly that is the most likely scenario. However it is not the only possibility: this could be a record of the witness of either Nicodemus or Joseph of Arimathea.

The chiastic placement of these sections that both involve a mention of a testimony is true, and an exhortation to believe may be designed to facilitate the principle of two or three witnesses. Today we think of witnesses solely as people but that was certainly not the way the ancient Hebrews thought. Objects we think of as inanimate, as lacking in sentience or self-awareness, were not necessarily seen that way in the world of long ago. God, after all, called on heaven and earth as witnesses;[64] and Joshua called on a stone as a witness.[65]

Even concepts we would today consider to be pure abstractions might qualify as witnesses. Paul, for example, in citing the Scripture, *'Every matter must be established by the testimony of two or three witnesses,'* was actually using the number of his visits to the Corinthians as his witnesses.

So, in line with this mode of thinking and presuming John is *'the one who saw it'* and also presuming he's the only one left alive who saw the crucifixion, he has used the poetic technique of chiasmus recalling the words of Jesus to confirm his testimony. The Spirit of Jesus is his second witness as he calls forth belief from his readers and encourages them to have faith not just in earthly things but also in heavenly ones.

---

64 Psalm 50:4
65 Joshua 24:27

3.4 The Breath of the Spirit

The wind blows where it wishes. You hear its sound, but you do not know where it comes from or where it is going. So it is with everyone born of the Spirit.

John 3:8^{BSB}

The soldiers came and broke the legs of the first man who had been crucified with Jesus, and those of the other.

John 19:32^{BSB}

IN THE BEGINNING IT WAS the breath of God that gave birth to humanity, changing mere clay into an in-spirited man. Jesus, in speaking to Nicodemus, seems like He has changed the topic—moving from a discussion of being born again to a focus on the unpredictable flow of the Holy Spirit. Yet, within Jewish thinking, the transition is a natural one: the Greek word 'pneuma', *the wind, spirit, breath,* is cognate with the Hebrew 'ruach', *wind, spirit, breath.*

Yet it is, surprisingly, not the 'ruach' of God that raised the first man from the dust. The word used for *breath* is 'nashamah':

And the Lord God formed man of the dust of the ground, and breathed into his nostrils the breath ['nashamah'] of life; and man became a living soul.

Genesis 2:7^{KJV}

Now 'nashamah' has similar connotations to 'ruach'. It means *puff* or *blast of wind, breath of life, soul, spirit, divine inspiration, vital intellect*. Despite coming from a root associated with the panting and travail of childbirth, Jewish sages across the ages have noted that it encodes the word for *name*. God breathes life into a child at conception, they say, by whispering a name. In naming us, He creates a soul and apportions to us our identity, destiny and inheritance.

So Jesus, naturally, speaks of the wind of the Spirit—the breath of God—in relation to the birth from above, the new birth, the time of being 'born again'. And here we see the significance of the unusual aspects of naming in John's text: names and birth are inextricably woven together. God gifts us a soul by speaking a name. He watches over our unformed body and ordains our days even before we were born.[66]

When we no longer have breath, we die. This is the significance of the chiasmus that John has put together for us. *'The soldiers came and broke the legs of the first man,'* he tells us in the mirror match. The purpose of breaking the legs of the condemned men was so that they could no longer push themselves up to catch a breath. They died quickly of suffocation.

But Jesus was already dead. It was not by human will that He breathed His last, but by His own will and that of the Father. We might be reminded at this point of the death of Moses:

> Moses the servant of the Lord died there in Moab, as the Lord had said. He buried him in Moab, in the valley opposite Beth Peor, but to this day no one knows where his grave is.
>
> Deuteronomy 34:5–6[NIV]

---

66 Psalm 139:16

The text seems to indicate that the Lord Himself buried Moses. Indeed some Jewish thinkers consider that God gently took the last breath of Moses with a kiss. His was a peaceful and calm death.[67] Although we cannot say the same of the death of Jesus, we can say that He was the One who laid down His life and who took it up again.[68] So, in the sense that He breathed His last in accordance with divine will and not because of the manipulations and machinations of a cabal of politically powerful elites, His death has similarities with that of Moses.

That's where the wind is blowing—the story of Moses. After all, Jesus explicitly mentioned him during His conversation with Nicodemus.

---

67 See, for example, myjewishlearning.com/article/kiss-of-death/ (accessed 9 November 2023)

68 John 10:18

3.5 The 'Twice-Born'

The fourth gospel begins at Bethany-beyond-the-Jordan where crowds were drawn to participate in an act of repentance under the direction of John the Baptiser. Jesus returned to this spot after forty days in the desert, was identified by John as the 'Lamb of God' and then spent the next few days conversing with various men who would eventually become His first disciples.

On the third day, the group set out for Galilee. Passing back over the Jordan, they would have come first to Scythopolis, the only city of the Decapolis on the west bank of the Jordan River. Scythopolis was an ancient city, originally known as Beit She'an. It was an Egyptian outpost at various times in its history; Anat was one of the deities worshipped there during those periods. It was resettled in the third century before Christ by Scythian mercenaries who were given the city by the Ptolemies, the Greek rulers of Egypt. They claimed descent from both the half-human half-god hero, Herakles, and from the wine-god Dionysius. Alleging Scythopolis was the birthplace of Dionysius, they claimed he'd buried his nursemaid Nysa there. Sometimes the city was called Scythopolis-Nysa to emphasise the connection.

As the disciples walked through the city en route to Cana, they could hardly have missed the massive temple there. And regardless of whether their conversation drifted to the legends of Dionysius and Herakles or not, those spiritual powers were certainly on Jesus' mind. As noted in *The Summoning of Time*, He took apart the claims of Dionysius the so-called 'True Vine' at Cana, and He dismissed the pretensions of Herakles during the episode when He cleansed the Temple of money-lenders.

However, Jesus wasn't entirely done with Dionysius. Not all of the titles stolen by the wine-god had been retrieved. There was a significant one that needed Jesus' specific attention. No doubt it was brought back to the apostle John's mind many years later because of the popularity of Dionysius in Ephesus.[69]

Now, in Greek mythology, Zeus had transformed himself into a serpent and ravished Persephone. She gave birth to a horned child known as Zagreus who was attacked and butchered by the Titans, the elder-gods who were eventually deposed by Zeus. The death of Zagreus was also the birth of Dionysius. Consequently Dionysius was called 'twice-born', an obvious counterfeit of the status of each follower of Jesus as 'born again' or 'born from above'.

The skirmish at Cana against Dionysius—and let's not forget Anat and Baal-Hadad in that conflict—was the opening battle in a prolonged war. There was Dionysius' claim to be able to grant the ability to his favourites to make wine from anything;[70] there was his claim to be the 'True Vine'; there was his claim to the title 'twice-born'. All these—like the claims of so many other godlings—had to be answered and their various liens dismissed. Jesus' war against Dionysius was just as intense as His policy of annihilation against Zeus and Baal-Hadad.

---

[69] Arthur George, *The Mythology of Wine*, Tellwell Talent 2020

[70] He was also, according to Ovid's *Metamorphoses*, the deity who bestowed the 'golden touch' on Midas.

No one has
ascended
into heaven

except the One
who descended
from heaven
—the Son of Man.

Just as Moses lifted up the snake
in the wilderness, so the Son of Man
must be lifted up, that everyone who
believes in Him may have eternal life.

John 3:13-15 BSB

Now these things happened
so that the Scripture would be fulfilled:
'Not one of His bones will be broken.'
And, as another Scripture says:
'They will look on the One
they have pierced.'

John 19:36-37 BSB

4.1 Ascent and Descent

> *No one has ascended into heaven except the One who descended from heaven—the Son of Man.*
>
> John 3:13^{BSB}

THIS IS AN EXTREMELY DIFFICULT STATEMENT. At first sight it seems straightforward and unequivocal. But, but, but—what about Elijah going up in a whirlwind? What about Enoch being taken? What about Moses and the seventy elders who went up to dine with God in a place with a sapphire pavement?

Now, the last two questions are not hard to reconcile with Jesus' statement. It's quite unclear where Enoch went and, in fact, it's even unclear whether God took him or the angels did.[71] As for Moses

---

[71] There are two slightly different words translated 'God' in Genesis 5:24^{NIV} —'*Enoch walked faithfully with God; then he was no more, because God took him away.*' The first is 'ha'elohim' and the second is 'elohim'. The word, 'elohim' is ambiguous and can mean *God, angels, spirits* and even *judges*. Michael Heiser considers it to designate *an inhabitant of the heavenly realms*. The word 'ha'elohim' simply means '*the* elohim'. I personally do not consider this to be ambiguous in the way 'elohim' is. I believe that every instance of 'ha'elohim' in Scripture refers to the angels, even in the phrase 'bene ha'elohim' which is usually translated *sons of God*, but I believe is more appropriately rendered *company of angels*. The translation of 'ha'elohim' consistently as *angels* has significant implications because it calls into question the identity of the divine being who asked Abraham to sacrifice Isaac. For more details on 'ha'elohim' as *angels*, see: *Dealing with Kronos: Spirit of Abuse and Time*, Armour Books 2022.

and the seventy elders, while the text says the pavement under God's feet looked like bright heaven, it doesn't say unambiguously that it *was* heaven. It's a different matter, however, when it comes to Elijah:

> *As they continued walking and talking, a chariot of fire and horses of fire separated the two of them, and Elijah ascended in a whirlwind into heaven.*
>
> 2 Kings 2:11[NRS]

This is quite problematical. Because, if we are going to be pedantic, then what about those angels that Jacob saw in a dream vision ascending and descending on a ladder between earth and heaven, while God was stationed at the top? We might try to wriggle out of this difficulty by suggesting that when Jesus said, 'No one,' He meant people, not angels. However, that's not the case. The Greek word here is a categorical denial that *anyone or anything* has ever ascended to heaven. What Jesus was stating was that no counter-example exists to invalidate His claim.

John is here picking up a thread that has been hanging loose since the first chapter: when Jesus spoke to Nathanael and said:

> *Very truly I tell you, you will see heaven open, and the angels of God ascending and descending on the Son of Man.*
>
> John 1:51[NIV]

That, as indicated in *The Elijah Tapestry*, is a chiastic match with the words of Jesus to the Magdalene:

> *Do not cling to me, for I have not yet ascended to the Father; but go to my brothers and say to them, 'I am ascending to my Father and your Father, to my God and your God.'*
>
> John 20:17[ESV]

Jesus is using the word 'ascended' here with the connotation of 'resurrected'. In fact, He clarified His statement to Nicodemus that no one had ever ascended to heaven with an explanation that He meant *ascended* in the sense of being *lifted up*, just as Moses lifted up the serpent in the wilderness. This term, *lifted up*, He then immediately linked to His coming death and resurrection.

His statement, *'No one has ascended into heaven except the One who descended from heaven—the Son of Man,'* is therefore an unqualified declaration that no one has been resurrected from the dead, except Himself.[72] And that, of course, raises its own problems because it's an assertion made long before He died. It doesn't make sense because it speaks of things yet to happen as if they have already occurred.

Yet, as indicated in *The Summoning of Time*, this is the message throughout John's second chapter: Jesus is not bound by time, He is its Lord and also its redeemer. He summons time as His servant, He is not captive to its constraints.

---

[72] Obviously there were some people who had been brought back to life throughout history but not resurrected. The difference between resurrection and being raised from the dead is that 'being raised' means the person can die again, but 'being resurrected' means death cannot happen again.

4.2 Lifted Up

THE DEATH OF JESUS OCCURRED at the Passover and His resurrection on the Feast of Firstfruits. The coming of the Holy Spirit coincided with the celebration of Shavuot, a festival that commemorated the giving of the Commandments at Mount Sinai. Almost universally overlooked in this lineup is the Ascension of Jesus—*ascension* now in its normal usage as His return to heaven when He was lifted up into the sky, a cloud caused Him to disappear from sight and a couple of angels asked His disciples why they kept staring skywards instead of getting on with what Jesus had asked them to do.

Surely, if every other major event at this time in the life of Jesus is paralleled in Exodus, the Ascension is too. Yes, there is such an event—and it's all about lifting up into the sky as well:

> *The Amalekites fought Israel at Rephidim. Moses said to Joshua, 'Choose some of our men. Then fight the Amalekites. Tomorrow I will stand on top of the hill. I will hold in my hand the staff God told me to take along.' Joshua did as Moses told him and fought the Amalekites, while Moses, Aaron, and Hur went to the top of the hill. As long as Moses held up his hands, Israel would win, but as soon as he put his hands down, the Amalekites would start to win. Eventually, Moses' hands felt heavy. So Aaron and Hur took*

a rock, put it under him, and he sat on it. Aaron held up one hand, and Hur held up the other. His hands remained steady until sunset. So Joshua defeated the Amalekite army in battle.

The Lord said to Moses, 'Write this reminder on a scroll, and make sure that Joshua hears it, too: I will completely erase any memory of the Amalekites from the earth.' Moses built an altar and called it THE LORD IS MY BANNER. *He said, 'Because a hand was lifted against the Lord's throne, He will be at war against the Amalekites from one generation to the next.'*

Exodus 17:8–16^{GWT}

The name of the altar Moses built, 'Yahweh-Nissi', *God My Banner*, has deeper connotations than a flag or a battle-standard. 'Nissi' derives from 'nes', *lift up*, also denoting *forgiveness, miracle* and *draw forth*.

Furthermore it's the word for a pole and is found again in the story about serpents attacking the Israelites in the wilderness. To save the people. the Lord instructed Moses:

Make a fiery serpent and set it on a pole, and everyone who is bitten, when he sees it, shall live.

Numbers 21:8^{ESV}

This is the incident that Jesus was referring to when He said:

Just as Moses lifted up the snake in the wilderness, so the Son of Man must be lifted up, that everyone who believes in Him may have eternal life.

John 3:14–15^{BSB}

The people had been grumbling about the lack of food and water, dishonouring and blaming both God and Moses. Fire-serpents—a natural-world equivalent to the spiritual realm's burning seraphim who guard the honour of God's throneroom—attacked the people. God's remedy was to instruct Moses to make a copper serpent, to raise it on a pole, and to tell the people to gaze upon it so they would be healed. Yet, the words of God imply more than simply lifting up the image on a *pole*, they equally say for Moses to lift it up on a *miracle*.

This foreshadowing of the death of Jesus for the healing of the world was a miraculous sign. In fact, *sign* is another possible translation of 'nes', *pole* and *miracle*—ironic since John avoids the Greek word *miracle* in favour of *sign*.

4.3 The Highway of Angels

BACK IN JOHN'S FIRST CHAPTER, Jesus told Nathanael:

> *You will all see heaven open and the angels of God going up and down on the Son of Man, the one who is the stairway between heaven and earth.*
>
> John 1:51[NLT]

This is a reference to the vision of Jacob at Luz:[73]

> *He had a dream in which he saw a stairway resting on the earth, with its top reaching to heaven, and the angels of God were ascending and descending on it.*
>
> Genesis 28:12[NIV]

The Hebrew word, 'sullam', *stairway* or *ladder*, is only found here in Scripture. It comes from the root 'sulal', *to lift up* or *exalt*. In a rare case of different languages having congruent nuances surrounding their corresponding words, the Greek word 'hupsoó' used to describe the *lifting up* of the serpent in the wilderness also means *exalted*.

Yet there's an even earlier reference to *lifting up* in John's gospel, once again relating to 'sullam'. When the Baptiser is quizzed

---

[73] Renamed Bethel (*House of God*) by Jacob after this dream.

about his identity, he finally answers with a quote from the prophet Isaiah:

> *The voice of one crying in the wilderness: 'Prepare the way of the Lord; make straight in the desert a highway for our God.*
>
> Isaiah 40:3[NKJV]

That word, *highway*, is 'mesillah' from 'sulal', *lifted up*. In ancient days, a highway literally was *high*; it was built up above the surrounding terrain.[74] In the *Song of Deborah*, 'mesillah' is often translated *courses*. The *'stars in their courses,'* she sang, *'fought against Sisera.'*[75] Deborah's triumph was not just against earthly foes, but against the spiritual forces of Anat[76] and her seventy brothers, the 'young lions' of the nations.

Just as Jacob saw angels ascending and descending on a 'sullam', Deborah saw stars—symbolic of angels—racing along a 'mesillah' to war against Anat.

By John's third chapter, we find a steady theme emerging: that of lifting up. He's been overt in mentioning the *highway* of Isaiah and the *stairway* of Jacob, and he's been subtle in the reference to the star *courses* of Deborah who triumphed over Anat. At the end of the gospel, we find another subtle reference to the lifting up of the 'sullam'—in a scene redolent of Anat when Jesus says to Mary the Magdalene, *'Do not touch Me for I have not yet ascended to My Father.'*

This was an echo of the words of the high priest on Yom Kippur, the Day of Atonement, before he entered the Holy of Holies. He

---

74 In Isaiah 35:8, 'meslul' is *highway*.
75 Judges 5:20KJV
76 See: Anne Hamilton, *The Summoning of Time: John 2 and 20*, Armour Books 2024 or *Dealing with Lilith: Spirit of Dispossession*, Armour Books 2024

would chant over and over: 'Do not touch me with anything of this world, for I have not yet been with the Father.'[77]

John the Baptiser was the herald prophesied by Isaiah, calling out to announce the Messiah's coming along the highway of righteousness. But as John the apostle makes increasingly clear: *Jesus is the highway.* Just as the highway was the way that was lifted up, Jesus was the Way, the Truth and the Life lifted up for the salvation of the world.

---

77   See: larryhuchministries.com/blog/the-feast-of-yom-kippur/ (accessed 4 April 2024)

4.4 Drawing Water

Moses could never divest himself of his Egyptian upbringing and take on the fullness of his Hebrew heritage. By contrast, his foster-mother, Pharaoh's daughter, covenanted with the people of Israel and even took on the name, Bithiah, *daughter of Yahweh*. She was able to do the very thing Moses continually shied away from—taking on a Hebrew identity through accepting a Hebrew name. Moses, after all, is Egyptian, meaning *drawn from the water*. Based on its similarity to other Egyptian names, it encodes a dedication to the river Nile. Pharaoh's daughter in dubbing him 'Moses' placed him under the protection of the river-god. Or perhaps she was thinking more of a river goddess.

In *The Summoning of Time*, I made a case for identifying Bint-Anat, *daughter of Anat*, as 'Pharaoh's daughter' who is unnamed throughout the Exodus saga but appears as Bithiah in the genealogies of 1 Chronicles 4. Anat was a Canaanite goddess, the particular favourite of Rameses the Great, who named not only his daughter Bint-Anat after his patron, but also his dog, his horse and his sword.

An inescapable sub-strata of John's gospel involves the conflict between Jesus and Anat. Her claims to have defeated even Death itself were a challenge He did not ignore. Throughout the second and second-last chapters He responds definitively to both Anat and her brother, Baal-Hadad, the cloud-rider, despoiling every part of the liturgy and myth associated with them.

Still, here in third chapter of John's gospel, we find that subtle allusions to Anat are still prevalent. Although Rameses II looked for defence and security to a foreign goddess, there was in fact a homegrown version of the savage Canaanite warrior princess, Anat. This was Neith 'the terrifying'. Her Greek counterpart was seen to be the war goddess Athena, and her Carthaginian equivalent to be Tanit.[78]

In the background of both the third and the third-last chapter, Neith is a lurking presence that Jesus has taken on in mortal combat. To see how true that is, it's necessary to look at Neith's claims.

Neith, it was alleged, invented birth and gave life to humanity. She was also there at a person's death to help them adjust to the afterlife. She helped to dress the dead and open the way for them to paradise in the 'Field of Reeds'. She is described as a goddess of the cosmos, fate, wisdom, water, rivers, mothers, childbirth, hunting, war and weaving. Woven bandages and linen shrouds were considered her gifts since her divine power was mediated through wrapping the deceased body. She was considered androgynous, and was sometimes depicted as having three heads—lion, woman and serpent—very much like the angelic cherubim. She is said to have created the world by speaking seven magical words, to have woven all of existence into being and to have judged amongst the gods who was worthy of the kingship. At the Temple of Neith, this inscription was recorded: 'I am all that has been, that is, and that will be. No mortal has yet been able to lift the veil that covers me.'[79]

---

78 The name 'Tanit' may simply mean *land of Nit* or *land of Neith*. Given Neith's association with water, this might be the sea, thus connecting with Hebrew 'tan', *sea monster*.

79 See: en.m.wikipedia.org/wiki/Neith and www.worldhistory.org/Neith/ (accessed 10 November 2023)

Apart from hunting and war, and the veil,[80] every aspect and attribute of Neith has been addressed in the opening and closing chapters of John's gospel. Even the Field of Reeds—since, after all, Cana means *reeds*. Even the multi-headed cherubim, both during the episode of cleansing the Temple in the second chapter and the positioning of the angelic guardians in the tomb in the second-last chapter. In addition, perhaps not even hunting and war are really overlooked, since one of her symbols is a pair of crossed arrows, and her Greek counterpart Athena is regularly depicted holding a spear—the weapon that pierced the side of Jesus.

So many of Neith's claims are a direct affront to Yahweh, a declaration that He copied her, that Jesus could not leave her allegations unanswered. Yet the very fact He responded to the claims suggests they had some legitimacy. What spiritual legal right did Neith have in the lives of everyday Jews? Did it have something to do with the fact that Moses might have been taken out of Egypt, but Egypt had never been taken out of him? And had his misplaced loyalty affected all the long history of Israel, right up to the time of Jesus?

Moses, named *drawn from the water* and dedicated to the Nile, was—as a child—almost certainly placed under the protection of Neith. After all, *drawn from the waters* of the river, *drawn from the waters* of childbirth, *drawn from the waters* of the Nile whose source was guarded by Neith all evoke this river-and-childbirth goddess. She, after all, was the local version of Anat—and, if his adoptive mother was indeed Bint-Anat, this would have been seen as simply bringing him under the same spiritual guardianship.

---

80   John doesn't need to mention the ripping of the veil in the Temple—every other evangelist did so, as well as the writer of the epistle to the Hebrews. It's common knowledge that does not require an explicit reference in order to still be included as part of the story.

Now Pharaoh's daughter prophesied over the child she brought up in the palace. Every name is a prophecy, a calling to fulfil a destiny prepared for us, an activation of identity, a dedication for the future. It's the child's choice to take this on—or not—but names are not simply labels. They are fuses to ignite the blessing of God from whom all names ultimately come.

So the prophecy of Pharaoh's daughter pointed to that amazing miracle when Moses, leading the people of Israel and pursued by the armies of Pharaoh, was able to draw the Hebrews safely from the waters of the Red Sea. However—*drawn from the water* is not the name God wanted for Moses. It wasn't a divine choice. It was a human one.

On Mount Sinai, during Moses' turning aside to see the bush that was burning but never consumed, God offered him a name covenant. As mentioned previously, this involves an exchange: both a new and hitherto-unrevealed name for God as well as a new name for the person God is inviting into covenant. God, of course, famously revealed Himself to Moses as I AM WHO I AM. (This is, in fact, not 'Yahweh', despite the popularisation of that name as the one revealed to Moses. 'Yahweh' is *He is who He is* and is a clever concealment of the true sacred name. 'Ehyeh' is what God told Moses.)

Now, although God invited Moses to a name covenant at Mount Sinai, he didn't take up the offer. It's not obvious in English translation that God is doing this. It's only when we look at other instances in Scripture—Abraham, Sarah, Israel, Gideon, Phinehas, Peter, Paul—that we can begin to understand the nature of the different poetic modes involved.

During the encounter at the burning bush, God repeatedly asks Moses, *'What is it…?'* in reference to the things in his hand. Now Moses is 'Moseh' in Hebrew and *'What is it…?'* is 'mazeh'. The 'mazeh' in his hand is, by turns, a staff, a snake and a leprous condition. Much later in the Exodus epic, the *what-is-it* will be the manna that falls each day to sustain the people in the wilderness. But to begin with, it was Moses' trusty, reliable staff that had just morphed into a snake.

Now Moses' staff wasn't just the stick he leaned on—it also represented his vocation and his security. With it, he protected the flock and himself. So when God told him to throw it down, he was asking Moses to let go of the identity, the defences and the sanctuary he'd created for himself.

The staff also symbolised the ideal qualifications for God's call. As the symbol of a desert shepherd, it indicated Moses could herd sheep in a dangerous wilderness. He knew the weather signs, the location of wells and oases, the hostile wildlife—snakes, scorpions, jackals and foxes. However that shape-change of his staff to a serpent said something else.

In the centre of a Pharaoh's double crown sat a cobra—the emblem of the royal house. So that serpent says to Moses: you have the upbringing that will enable you to negotiate and navigate through the protocols of the Egyptian court. The leprosy indicates an attitude of grumbling—a cramping of the soul as it turns from God's call.

So Moses says 'no' to God's offer of a name exchange. And then he backs it up with another 'no'. And another. And another. And another. And to make it absolutely clear to God that 'no' means 'no', a few days later he undertakes a threshold covenant with an enemy of God. This forfeits all his protection from God as his covenant defender. In fact, it sets God implacably against him:

> *On the way to Egypt, at a place where Moses and his family had stopped for the night, the Lord confronted him and was about to kill him.*
>
> Exodus 4:24^{NLT}

This is one of the most mysterious incidents in all Scripture. Why would God commission Moses and then immediately try to kill him? To understand the significance of what transpires here, we have to realise Moses had just repeatedly refused God's invitation to a covenant. Still he'd headed off for Egypt but en route he took lodging that, in some way, involved treachery. Apparently he'd covenanted with an Egyptian deity—thereby derailing the Exodus before it even began.

Forty days after the first Passover in Egypt, God changed tactics. He again summonsed Moses to a name covenant but this time with a different twist. In the aftermath of the battle against the Amalekites, Moses called the Lord by a new name that had been revealed to him: Yahweh Nissi, *God my banner*. The word 'nissi' is related to 'nes', *sign, miracle, standard*, and is derived from *lift up, lift off, carry, bear armour, draw forth*.[81] Its source is in fact a Hebrew form of Moses, but without the inbuilt dedication to Neith and the river Nile. But still Moses was resistant to the exchange God offered.

Forty years later, he was still holding back on whole-hearted commitment to God. Every single day, manna, *what-is-it*, appeared to remind him God was still inviting him to a name covenant. From time to time, God would appear at the tent door, speaking to Moses *as to a friend*—some of the most tragic words in all Scripture. Moses apparently never invited Him in—because that would constitute covenant.

---

81 See: abarim-publications.com/Meaning/Massa.html (accessed 26 August 2024

And finally, after more than twelve thousand invitations that had been quietly ignored, Moses did the unthinkable. He publicly snubbed God. He hit a rock. Now, to us today, striking a stone doesn't mean much at all other than as an expression of frustration and annoyance. However, to the people of Israel it had a profound symbolic significance. To strike a rock meant to refuse covenant. And that covenant was once again about Moses' name: God was asking him to *draw water* by speaking, to no longer be *drawn from the water*. It was once again a call to forgo his allegiance with Egypt and to bond fully with the people and God of Israel. The Promised Land was not for the Egyptians, it was for the Hebrews and for those who covenanted with them.

This is why God denied Moses entry to the land. Because he simply would not surrender his Egyptian identity.[82] He could not inherit while still rejecting covenant with God, and maintaining loyalty to the river-god.

The tragedy of Moses is that, despite the greatness of his leadership, his enormous sacrifices over four decades, his incredible bravery, his obedience to God and the miracles of faith he participated in, he was still double-minded. He simply couldn't trust God enough to accept the covenant on offer. He wanted the inheritance on his own terms.

---

82   This inability to fully link himself with the Hebrew people may be reflected in his choice of a Cushite wife, after he'd sent away the mother of his sons, Zipporah. The word for *sent away* is the usual word for *divorce*, and while many commentators are desperate to avoid this conclusion, it's difficult to escape. The unnamed Cushite wife came from Upper Egypt, towards what is now the country of Sudan. Both Aaron and Miriam were appalled at Moses' choice, grumbling and complaining about it. As a consequence, Miriam became leprous—the usual physical symptom of a spiritually irritable, gossipy heart. Perhaps Aaron and Miriam had a point but they expressed it dishonourably. Just because the Hebrews were God's chosen people didn't mean He didn't love and care for the Egyptians.

When it came right down to it, he was little different to the rest of the Israelites. The golden calf in his heart was simply invisible, as opposed to the highly visible idol set up by his brother. But it was there nonetheless, and it only took two generations for it to emerge in the lives of his descendants.

He was 'stiff-necked', as the people of Israel were. And he was 'hard-hearted', just as Pharaoh was. He divorced Zipporah, his wife of forty years, and he sent her and his children away, and then later married a Cushite woman. Jesus said:

> *Because of your hardness of heart Moses allowed you to divorce your wives, but from the beginning it was not so.*
>
> Matthew 19:18^{ESV}

The words of Jesus have to apply to Moses' own divorce and his abandonment of his family. And, whether he intended it or not, Moses' actions sent consistent subtle messages about being a leader 'apart' rather than covenantally joined to God and His people:

- his children, not being with him, did not participate in the wandering of the Hebrews; they were set aside as different, not fully part of the people of Israel

- in choosing his wives—first a Midianite, then a Cushite—Moses married outside the Hebrew tribes. It is particularly significant that he maintained his Egyptian identity by taking a bride from Cush in Upper Egypt—an action massively criticised by his brother and sister

- given that manna fell six times a week for around forty years, Moses had around twelve thousand reminders from God that he'd been invited to a name covenant involving swapping out his Egyptian identity for a Hebrew one—and these twelve thousand occasions do not include the 'mazeh' or 'nissi' incidents or the many times God stood talking face-to-face with him, as with a friend, at the door of the Tent of Meeting but was never invited in.

Moses, like the rest of us, was a complex mixture of light and dark elements, of good and bad, loving and cruel. He was meek and yet impetuous, self-sacrificial and yet self-centred, caring and yet unyielding, brave and bold and yet also fearful.

For anyone inheriting the mantle of Moses, as I've suggested Nicodemus did, then there are three aspects that need mending before the unfinished tasks of Israel's greatest teacher can be addressed.

The first is the matter of drawing water in the right way, without refusing covenant. The second involves the name covenant itself. Nicodemus, as a result of asking God for water in an appropriate fashion, exchanged 'Buni' for 'Naqdimon', thereby accepting a name covenant and succeeding where Moses had blundered.

Nicodemus also demonstrated exceptional meekness throughout the entire process. Moses was said, in Numbers 12:3, to be the meekest of all men in the earth. Now, *meekness* in Scripture is not weakness but rather strength under control. Nicodemus demonstrated this character trait: when the official attempted to unsettle, perhaps even provoke, him with repeated demands for payment, Nicodemus remains unflustered, and under control.

The third aspect is the matter of *lift up* and *what-is-it*, the names God so often offered to Moses. When it comes right down to it and we recognise that what-is-it is manna, then at least part of the unfinished business for anyone inheriting the mantle of Moses is the provision of water and food

And the other part, connected to 'nissi', is a miracle in a time of war.

4.5 Nicodemus in the War with Rome

Throughout their wilderness wanderings, the people looked to Moses to provide water and food. Trouble arose when, instead of approaching God in faith and gratitude, they began murmuring and moaning. Moses himself became so irritated with their griping that, even after forty years, he still found himself frustrated when quarrels erupted over water. In his anger, he made clear what was in his heart. God had told him:

> *'Take the staff, and you and your brother Aaron gather the assembly together. Speak to that rock before their eyes and it will pour out its water. You will bring water out of the rock for the community so they and their livestock can drink.'*
>
> *So Moses took the staff from the Lord's presence, just as He commanded him. He and Aaron gathered the assembly together in front of the rock and Moses said to them, 'Listen, you rebels, must we bring you water out of this rock?' Then Moses raised his arm and struck the rock twice with his staff. Water gushed out, and the community and their livestock drank.*
>
> *But the Lord said to Moses and Aaron, 'Because you did not trust in Me enough to honour Me as holy in the sight of the Israelites, you will not bring this community into the land I give them.'*

Numbers 20:8–12^{NIV}

There's insult piled on insult in Moses' action. To see how profound it is, let's go back to the moment when God told Moses to take the staff. Now it transpires this wasn't just any staff, it was the one that was kept before the Presence of the Lord. It was therefore Aaron's staff—the rod stored inside the Ark of the Covenant.

Back when the people had grumbled about Moses showing favouritism to his brother Aaron, God had shown that Aaron was His choice of leader by causing his staff, and his alone, to simultaneously bud, flower and produce almonds. God had told Moses to keep this rod as a sign for the people about rebellion. It was a symbol of God's favour as well as a reminder of His warning: 'Don't rebel against Me!'

So Moses took this very special staff signifying, 'Don't rebel,' then gathered the assembly together, chastised them as 'you rebels' and, with all of them as witnesses, acted out his own rebellion. He defied God's instructions to him and, in the process, used a symbol of God's favour in leadership to tell God he wanted no part of a covenant. He abused a badge of authority by trashing every aspect of the meaning God had invested in it. The visual image that was supposed to be a reminder not to rebel against God was turned into a sign of exactly the opposite.

And then, when God took him at his word and withdrew the covenant invitation, he tried to bargain with God once he realised that getting precisely what he'd asked for meant that he couldn't enter the Promised Land.

All because he insisted on providing water by striking, not speaking.

Nicodemus does not make this mistake. He not only provides water by speaking to a human authority, he replenishes it by speaking to divine authority. He is humble, as Moses was reputed to be, when he prayed for rain—and then, when approaching

God for the impossible, he was completely audacious. His faith was bold and confident when he said, 'Show the world that You have favourites.'

And with those words, he evoked the action of God in causing the staff of Aaron to bud and bloom and bear almonds. Nicodemus, a governmental leader and a teacher in Israel, a Pharisee following the way of Moses, had reached the moment when the past could be mended. He could wear the mantle of Moses and, when the time of testing came, he could choose a different path. He accepted the name covenant that Moses never did. He saw the water, and the spirit, that flowed from the Rock—the Cornerstone that was Jesus Himself—and received his inheritance.

Now, about forty years after the death of Jesus, the Temple in Jerusalem was destroyed. Roman armies surrounded the capital and laid siege to it. In the lead-up to the final conflict, Nicodemus became one of the leaders of the so-called 'Peace Party'. Together with two wealthy friends,[83] he proposed a unique solution to the Roman menace: not to fight, not to surrender, but to simply beat the Romans by slow attrition.

Nicodemus and his friends proposed to feed the population of Jerusalem for an entire decade. They stockpiled food and grain for that very purpose. They wanted to shut up the city for as many years as it took the Romans, with their empire to defend, their frontiers to guard and their ever-smouldering political fires to douse, to decide the prize wasn't worth the price.

But what the friends hadn't counted on was the Zealots. Peace was not in the Zealot mindset. Freedom-fighters committed to an armed struggle against the Romans, the ranks of the Zealots

---

83 The names of the two friends were Kalba Sabbua' and Ben Zizit. See: jewishencyclopedia.com/articles/11526-nicodemus-nakdimon-ben-gorion (accessed 27 November 2023)

included the earliest known band of assassins, the dagger-wielding 'sicarii'. These killers targeted anyone they considered had abandoned the Jewish faith and become apostate, or else had collaborated with the enemy. Their reign of terror—reminiscent of Anat or Neith's influence—is thought to have included the murder of the high priest Jonathan, as well as Nicodemus' brother, also named Jonathan.

The Zealots did not want the peace plan proposed by Nicodemus and his friends to be even a remotely possible option. They therefore burned the entire stockpile of food that the trio had accumulated.

Like Moses, Nicodemus was God's agent for the provision of food for the people. In Moses' day, that was manna—delivered daily, for decades. In Nicodemus' day, he'd planned to deliver grain for an entire city for at least a decade. But he'd been betrayed and sabotaged by his own allies—since the Zealots, according to Josephus, were extremists within the sect of the Pharisees.

It's unknown what happened to Nicodemus. He may have escaped to Pella or to his estates at Rumah, near Cana, and finished his days in comparative peace. Or he may have perished in the siege of Jerusalem. We can't be sure either way.

Perhaps the greatest tragedy of his story is that, today in Israel, it's the first-century Zealots who are lionised as the heroes, not those of the Peace Party who devised a resistance plan involving neither fight, nor surrender. The Zealots made their last stand at the fortress of Masada—the very place where today the members of the Israeli Defence Force swear their oath, 'Never again.'

4.6 Eternal Life

The Son of Man must be lifted up, that everyone who believes in Him may have eternal life.

John 3:14–15[BSB]

Now these things happened so that the Scripture would be fulfilled: 'Not one of His bones will be broken.' And, as another Scripture says: 'They will look on the One they have pierced.'

John 19:36–37[BSB]

WHAT DOES 'ETERNAL LIFE' ACTUALLY MEAN?

There would have been a danger, at least in John's mind with his close-quarter understanding of the gap between contemporary Greek and Jewish culture, that 'eternal life' might simply be perceived as 'immortality of the soul'. This was a concept familiar to Greek thinking, and that many people believed in anyway. It wasn't a stretch of faith for most early Christians of Greek background to slot 'eternal life' smoothly into their pre-existing philosophical grid and view it in terms of an indestructible soul.

Yet there are different ways of viewing this. One, of course, is that the soul becomes disembodied but enjoys all the wonders of heaven forever and ever. Hence the sentiment even today that a deceased person has become an angel. An alternative view held by Christian adherents of a Gnostic or Pythagorean bent posited the transmigration of the soul—that, every century or so, the soul would be reincarnated in a different body. Sometimes an alleged memory of those previous lives would intrude when the person presently existing experienced something to bring the past back into recall.

According to the testimony of the early church, however, John wrote his gospel precisely in order to combat such erroneous ideas. The issue was the complete incompatibility of the concept of resurrection with that of reincarnation. Resurrection is a reunion of body and soul—enhanced body and purified soul, admittedly. However it is not an insertion of an old, mostly amnesiac, soul into a new body.

Many Gnostics believed that the spirit was good but that flesh was evil. The very idea of resurrection was anathema to them: they wanted their soul freed from the defilement of the flesh, not a regathering of body and spirit. Their idea that the flesh was created corrupt, instead of being one of the good gifts of God, had theological outworkings. Many Gnostics differentiated between 'Jesus' the man and 'the Christ' who was a spirit. Accordingly they believed that 'the Christ' descended on Jesus at His baptism but departed from Him before the crucifixion. Instead, a substitute had died in His place while He had stood to one side, laughing. In the Gnostic system, 'the Christ' was free of both the defilements of the flesh and their consequence, death.

John makes it clear through his chiasmus that 'eternal life' involves the body. And that, despite the philosophical slipway the Gnostics were trying to create for themselves, it was prophesied that the Messiah would die. The atonement was planned before the foundation of the world. Jesus didn't seek to evade death because He was the Author of Life, He sought to put an end to Death because He was the Resurrection and the Life.

John quoted Psalm 34:20 when he wrote, *'Not one of His bones will be broken,'* where David was talking about deliverance from his enemies. He wrote the psalm after he'd fled to Gath and, to protect himself again the Philistines, pretended to be mad. He drooled and clawed at the doors and the king sent him away. In context, this psalm is speaking about God delivering a person from death by honouring an act of subterfuge. Since this is exactly what some of the Gnostics said 'the Christ' had done—tricked His way out of death by replacing Himself with a look-alike substitute—and since John is at pains to deny it so strenuously, then he was evidently thinking about God's instructions regarding the sacrifice of the Passover Lamb:

> *Each Passover lamb must be eaten in one house. Do not carry any of its meat outside, and do not break any of its bones.*
>
> Exodus 12:46^{NLT}

The Hebrew word for *bones* here is highly nuanced. It means *self, substance, vitality, strength, life, entire being*. Not breaking any of those things is therefore a fitting juxtaposition with *'eternal life'* that Jesus spoke of to Nicodemus.

If any of the Gnostics were to suggest that John's choice of quotation from Psalm 34 supported their position, his next words put paid to that notion. He selects a verse from this passage in the writings of the prophet Zechariah:

> *They will look on Me, the One they have pierced. They will mourn for Him as one mourns for an only child, and grieve bitterly for Him as one grieves for a firstborn son.*
> *On that day the wailing in Jerusalem will be as great as the wailing of Hadad-rimmon in the plain of Megiddo.*
>
> Zechariah 12:10–11[BSB]

The prophecy not only points to Jesus as the Pierced One, it also—in combination with the prophecy of Daniel—points to the Son of Man as the Pierced One.

> *I saw One like the Son of Man coming with the clouds of heaven. He approached the Ancient of Days and was led into His presence.*
>
> Daniel 7:13^{BSB}

As pointed out in *The Summoning of Time*, Jesus was challenged for the right to come with the clouds of heaven. The storm-god Baal-Hadad, chief of the Canaanite pantheon, who was commonly called Rimmon by the Israelites, claimed the title of 'Cloud-rider'. Both names, Hadad and Rimmon, are mentioned in Zechariah's prophecy in connection with the Pierced One.

Like Elijah's contest against the prophets of Baal—clearly Hadad, since the challenge is actually about rain-bringing—Jesus warred against the so-called 'Cloud-rider', promising the high priest Caiaphas that he would see:

> *the Son of Man sitting at the right hand of power, and coming on the clouds of heaven.*
>
> Matthew 26:64^{NASB}

It was this statement, as Michael Heiser points out, that Caiaphas seized on to have Jesus condemned.[84] Just about everyone in those days knew what this announcement implied: to sit at the right hand of power meant to claim equality with God.

In this declaration, Jesus was simply making explicit what had been implicit all along: ever since He told Nicodemus He was the Son of Man, He'd been declaring He was part of the Godhead. In fact, prior to this, He'd told Nathanael, one of the first disciples to

---

84 See: Michael S Heiser, *The Unseen Realm: Recovering the supernatural worldview of the Bible,* Lexham Press 2015

follow Him, that he would see angels ascending and descending on the Son of Man.

From the very start Jesus revealed Himself as the One lifted up, the ladder to heaven, the highway to God and the bridge to eternal life to be accessed through believing faith.

4.7 Compunction

IN THE FOURTH CENTURY, AN ASCETIC movement developed, bringing to the church a deep need for intensive prayer and self-discipline. Many believers retired to the desert to devote themselves to a deeper focus on God. One of the spiritual correctives they emphasised was *compunction*, from 'punctio', *pierce*.

Compunction meant being *pierced to the heart* by the consciousness of one's sin. It was exemplified by those three thousand believers who were saved on the Day of Pentecost when Peter finished his speech:

> *'Let all the house of Israel know for certain that God has made Him both Lord and Christ—this Jesus whom you crucified.'*
>
> *Now when they heard this, they were pierced to the heart, and said to Peter and the rest of the apostles, 'Brothers, what are we to do?'*
>
> *Peter said to them, 'Repent, and each of you be baptised in the name of Jesus Christ for the forgiveness of your sins; and you will receive the gift of the Holy Spirit.'*
>
> Acts 2:36–38[NASB]

The wind that Jesus told Nicodemus would blow where it wished had come in fire and foreign tongues. It was piercing hearts spiritually, as once Jesus' side had been pierced physically.

Unless we are willing to repent—not simply to change our minds but to turn back to God—then the lustral waters of baptism mean nothing. They are a hollow sign, devoid of power because we have covered ourselves with self-righteousness rather than the righteousness of Jesus. We can't bear to accept the grace of repentance because the cost to our self-esteem is too high. We'd rather hang on to our tatters of pride, defending the last remnants of our dignity against any assault than admit to any wrong-doing.

Compunction is the piercing awareness of guilt—for which the remedy is repentance; repentance empowered by the atoning sacrifice of Jesus. It's a simple acknowledgment of sin and an acceptance of the grace to change and turn back to look upon the face of God.

Guilt is our friend.

Shame is not.

Guilt invites us to an awareness that we *did* wrong; shame insists we *are* wrong. Guilt speaks to our behaviour; shame speaks to our identity. Facing this intolerable conflict, shame therefore tries to substitute self-righteousness for the righteousness of Christ. Adam hastily sewed together some fig-leaves from the tree whose fruit he'd eaten, but God's covering for shame entailed sacrifice from the first.

Guilt is different from shame. Guilt is able to appropriate the blessings Jesus has won on the Cross and to clothe itself in His righteousness. Guilt may decide not to, and to fall off the cliff and become warped into shame instead; but it's rare for shame to climb the cliff, become guilt and recognise the sin is not the sinner.

Guilt is given to us so we will seek reconciliation through confession, repentance and forgiveness. Shame, however, seeks vindication along with the reassurance that its covering of self-righteousness *doesn't look* self-righteous.

Shame can forgive—because, after all, forgiveness says the other person wronged me. But shame can't repent—because, in a shame-based system, that means I *am* wrong, not that I *did* wrong. And I'm already in desperate denial about the fact I believe there's something essentially wrong in the very core of who I am, so I can't even consider repentance.

A failure to process shame is at the root of addiction and narcissism.[85] Yet Jesus will take all our shame, if we let Him, and He'll cover us, if we let Him. And He'll hide us in the wound in His side, if we let Him, and there'll He'll let us be born again in the breaking forth of water and the Spirit.

---

85 For a look at the connection between Anat and the blocking of the processing of shame—leading to narcissism or addiction—see: Anne Hamilton, *Dealing with Lilith: Spirit of Dispossession*, Armour Books 2024

4.8 Archimedes

Surprise, surprise! Archimedes is back.

The first two books in this series, *The Elijah Tapestry* and *The Summoning of Time*, both look at John's allusions to Archimedes and try to come to grips with them.

A decade ago, when a first faint niggle tugged at my mind that John's gospel hinted at a wrestle between Christianity and Archimedes, I looked for evidence of this unexpected contention. Now it isn't hard to find commentators talking about John's opposition to the Gnostics, and thus to the Pythagoreans within their ranks. Many also compare and contrast John's writings with those of Plato. But Archimedes? No. If there are scholars who have unearthed some clue that a battle royale was going on in the first century between supporters of Archimedes and Christian believers, I haven't found their work yet. However, there's definitely a battle in progress.

Let me briefly outline the life of Archimedes, mentioning the points salient to John's gospel, before I enumerate the allusions to him I've been able to find.

Archimedes lived in the third century before Christ and was born in Syracuse on the island of Sicily. His name means *master planner* or *master counsellor*.[86] He is considered the greatest mathematician, inventor and scientist of the ancient world. Many people are willing to concede he was probably the greatest ever. He found an approximation for π, the ratio between the diameter and circumference of a circle, that is still used when a calculator is not available. He found that $^{265}/_{153}$ was a good approximation for the square root of 3 by using the geometry of intersecting circles. The intersection looked like a fish,[87] so Archimedes called 153 the 'measure of the fish'.

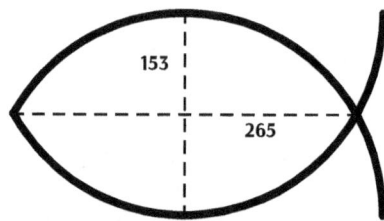

He is famous for his discovery of the principle of buoyancy. Tasked by the king with determining whether the gold in a crown had been adulterated with silver—but without damaging the crown in any way—Archimedes had an inspiration while getting into a bath. On realising the solution, he rushed out of the baths, yelling, 'Eureka! *I have found it!*'

He created a screw for raising water, designed machines for catapulting fiery missiles during battle, and developed the concept of the lever. He is famously reputed to have said, 'Give me a lever and a place to stand and I will move the world.' In his treatise, *The Sand Reckoner*, he estimated both the size of the universe and the number of grains of sand that would fit into it, concluding that both were finite—though obviously very large.

---

86   Was this therefore a title given to someone who had proved himself a master inventor and strategist? Or did his parents dub him this with hope and blessing?

87   In the centuries since, others have thought it looked like an almond or an eye and named it accordingly; however Archimedes does have precedence.

Archimedes died during the siege of Syracuse, allegedly killed by a Roman soldier. He was said to have been drawing on the ground and his last words were, 'Do not disturb my circles.'

The allusions to Archimedes in John's gospel fall into two categories:

- definite associations
- vague back-ups

The vague back-ups could easily be dismissed except for the definite associations that anchor them. Here are some of the references, most of which have been mentioned in previous books.

- 153 fish, recorded in John 21:11 as being caught on the third occasion Jesus met with His disciples after the resurrection. 153 as the 'measure of the fish' associated with $\sqrt{3}$ indicates this as a definite reference to Archimedes.

- Also in John 21, in the very last verse of the entire gospel, there is a reference to *The Sand Reckoner*, clearly contradicting the conclusion of Archimedes about the finiteness of all things. One of the first uses of the word 'kosmos' as meaning *universe* was by Archimedes,[88] thus John's use of the word 'kosmos' here while indicating that the books about what Jesus did are without limit and essentially infinite in extent, seems a clear thrust at Archimedan thought.

---

88 It is thought that Pythagoras was the first to use 'kosmos' in this sense, followed by Archimedes. (See: patrickcomerford.com/2014/01/john-1-29-42-who-is-christ-for-you-who.html – accessed 14 November 2023) However, the works of Pythagoras were only compiled several centuries after his death. Thus Archimedes may well have precedence.

The Greek word 'kosmos' means *well-ordered* or the *created order*, and is opposite to the concept of chaos. It gives us words like *cosmetic* and *cosmonaut*.

- As detailed in *The Summoning of Time*, there's an incredibly subtle pair of chiastic allusions to Archimedes in the second and second-last chapters. The first is the reference to the money-changers in the Temple who used Archimedes' buoyancy principle to check the Temple shekels for fakes. In the matching chiastic position, John and Peter view the grave-clothes in the tomb. Jesus has left the tomb, just as Archimedes left his bath.

- In John 12:14, the disciples are looking for a donkey that Jesus has charged them with finding. 'Eureka!' is the word they use on spotting it.[89] There are many variations on *eureka* in the gospels to do with finding things, so this particular link to Archimedes cannot be placed in the *definite* category.

- In John 8:6–8, it describes Jesus writing on the ground, just as Archimedes was reported to be doing when he died.

Now, of course, the most famous saying of Archimedes, at least as it has come down to us, is: 'Give me a lever and a place to stand and I will move the earth.' If John really was targeting Archimedes, then surely there would be a reference to this iconic statement. A search for 'lever', however, turns up a blank throughout the entire New Testament.

Now, as it transpires, the original words of Archimedes were a little less specific than 'lever'. According to Diodorus Siculus, his actual words were, 'Shall I go somewhere and move the whole earth with the lifting tool?'[90]

---

89 See: kingjamesbibleonline.org/John-12-14_meaning/ (accessed 21 March 2024)

90 Diodorus Siculus Hist., Bibliotheca historica Book 26, chapter 18, section 1, line 34

> *Just as Moses lifted up the snake in the wilderness, so the Son of Man must be lifted up.*
>
> John 3:14^{NIV}

If we replace our modern term *lever* with the ancient *lifting tool*, then along with all the other subtle and not-so-subtle allusions here, Jesus was making an oblique reference to the words of Archimedes. The Cross is the ultimate 'lifting tool' that will move the earth—and, more than the earth, the universe too. That's what Jesus was telling Nicodemus.[91] Because as Jesus went on immediately to tell him, 'God loved the cosmos so much that He gave His one and only Son…'

The prayers of Jesus our mediator are what change the world. It is the Cross, when lifted up, that lifts us up and enables all of the heavy lifting of prayer to be done by Jesus on our behalf.

The allusions to Archimedes, particularly the 'lifting tool' in the dialogue between Jesus and Nicodemus raise an interesting possibility. Is Nicodemus deliberately positioned by John as a counterpoint and contrast to Archimedes? Archimedes, after all, was famous for all the various weaponry he produced for the city of Syracuse to defeat various attacking navies—a claw to grab and grapple a ship, a heat ray that focussed a beam of light to set sails ablaze, vastly improved catapults with much greater striking accuracy. Nicodemus, on the other hand, prepared for war through provision, not of weaponry, but of necessary food stocks.

---

[91] Nicodemus belongs to the Jewish ruling council and thus was a counsellor to the government, just as Archimedes was.

4.9 Into the Curse

Jesus has many titles sprinkled throughout the gospels. But the most common are the 'Son of—' variants.

He is called the 'Son of Man' 79 times[92] and 'Son of God' 22 times—plus five variants.[93] 'Son of the Most High God' was generally used in Gentile territory since Yahweh was referenced as 'Most High' outside the borders of Israel to indicate that, although there were other deities, He was recognised in some quarters as supreme.

Besides these titles, there were two Messianic designations—'Son of David' for the royal messiah and 'Son of Joseph' for the war messiah. John never uses the expression 'Son of David' and he is the only gospel writer to use 'Son of Joseph' as a title, rather than in genealogical terms.

---

[92] *Matthew* 8:20; 9:6; 10:23; 11:19; 12:8; 12:32; 12:40; 13:37; 13:41; 16:13; 16:27; 16:28; 17:9; 17:12; 17:22; 19:28; 20:18; 20:28; 24:27; 24:30; 24:37; 24:39; 24:44; 25:31; 26:2; 26:24; 26:45; 26:64

Mark 2:10; 2:28; 8:31; 8:38; 9:9; 9:12; 9:31; 10:33; 10:45; 13:26; 14:21; 14:41; 14:62; 15:39

Luke 5:24; 6:5; 6:22; 7:34; 9:22; 9:26; 9:44; 9:58; 11:30; 12:8; 12:10; 12:40; 17:22; 17:24; 17:26; 17:30; 18:8; 18:31; 19:10; 21:27; 21:36; 22:22; 22:48; 22:69; 24:7

John 1:51; 3:13; 3:14; 5:27; 6:27; 6:53; 6:62; 8:28; 9:35; 12:23; 12:34; 13:31

[93] *Matthew* 4:3; 4:6; 8:29; 14:33, 16:16 *(Son of the living God)*; 26:63; 27:40; 27:43; 27:54

Mark 1:1; 3:11; 5:7 *(Son of the Most High God)*; 15:3

Luke 1:32 *(Son of the Most High)*; 1:35; 4:3; 4:9; 4:41; 8:28 *(Son of the Most High God)*; 22:70

John 1:49; 3:18 *(God's one and only Son)*; 5:25; 10:36; 11:27; 19:7; 20:31

The phrase 'Son of David' is used 15 times in total by Matthew, Mark and Luke,[94] while 'Son of Joseph' is twice used by John.[95] The title 'Son of Joseph' had special connotations in the first century. At that time there was a widespread expectation that the vision of Zechariah about four craftsmen[96] was a prophecy of three messianic deliverers plus, as the fourth, a herald who would announce their coming. The traditional belief was that the herald would be the Elijah-who-is-to-come who would prepare the way for the other craftsmen. Following swiftly after him would be the royal messiah, the war messiah and the priestly messiah.

No one apparently anticipated that the royal messiah, the war messiah and the priestly messiah would be one and the same person.

Because the war messiah was expected to come from the tribe of Joseph—usually through Ephraim—he was dubbed 'Son of Joseph'. The concept of a war messiah went back to the notion of a priest anointed for war. Now there's a tendency to think of Joshua being in charge of Israel's armies during the time of the desert wanderings. However, that was not *always* the case:

> *Moses sent them to the war, one thousand from every tribe, with Phinehas son of Eleazar the priest, who was in charge of the holy articles and the signal trumpets.*
>
> Numbers 31:6[NET]

The Targums[97] describe Phinehas, the grandson of Aaron, as the priest 'anointed for war'—or as the war messiah who led the armies in battle. He was not from the tribe of Joseph, but a Levite in the line of Aaron. His main association with Joseph was that,

---

94 *Matthew* 1:1; 9:27; 12:23; 15:22; 20:30; 20:31; 21:9; 21:15; 22:42
    Mark 10:47; 10:48; 12:35
    Luke 18:38; 18:39; 20:41
95 *John* 1:45; 6:42
96 *Zechariah* 1:20

on entering the Promised Land, he took up residence in the hill country of Ephraim.

Now it's perilously easy to get the wrong impression about Phinehas, his zeal for God and the reasons he would have been appointed as a war leader.

The Israelites were nearing the end of their forty-year desert trek when they camped near the ancient site of Sodom. A plague broke out—the people had broken their covenant with Yahweh and had pledged themselves in a new covenant to the Baal of Peor. They did so by engaging in ritual prostitution with the priestesses of this *lord of the opening* and eating food sacrificed to the idol. They had therefore come out from under the covering of God's protection. God had withdrawn His presence. Plague had killed 24,000 people.

There is no question the assembly understood its origin—the very Hebrew word for *plague* here is derived from *smiting* or *hitting*, an action that when associated with *striking* a stone symbolised *refusing* or *violating covenant*.

As the people were weeping, a prince of Simeon sauntered into camp with one of the priestesses of Baal-Peor:

> *When Phinehas... saw this, he left the assembly, took a spear in his hand and followed the Israelite into the* **tent**. *He drove the spear into both of them... Then the plague against the Israelites was stopped; but those who died in the plague numbered 24,000.*

---

97   By the end of the first century, professional translators were reading the Hebrew Scriptures in whatever commonly spoken everyday language was in local usage. Even many Jews did not understand Hebrew. These translators added in explanatory comments and examples and their readings ended up similar to sermons. Originally it was forbidden to write down a 'targum' spoken by a translator, but in time this rule was relaxed.

> *The Lord said to Moses, 'Phinehas… has turned My anger away from the Israelites. Since he was as zealous for My honour among them as I am, I did not put an end to them in My zeal. Therefore tell him I am making My covenant of peace with him. He and his descendants will have a covenant of a lasting priesthood, because he was zealous for the honour of his God and made atonement for the Israelites.'*
>
> Numbers 25:7–13[NIV]

It would be extremely easy to view this incident as licensing moral vigilantes. It appears God approves violence, especially when it is invoked in the cause of His honour and holiness. But see that word emphasised in bold? *Tent*. Now the usual word for *tent*, 'ohel', is extremely common in Scripture and is mentioned well over three hundred times. This is *not* the usual word. In fact, 'qubbah' is never elsewhere translated as *tent*. It only happens here—*just* here—*just* this once. Normally 'qubbah' is associated with *curse*.

I remain continually astonished that 'qubbah' is rendered *tent* and that translators follow tradition, failing to sense the monumental theological implications of *curse*. It's a stunning foreshadowing of the work of Jesus. Here's a man going into a curse and coming out the other side, not with its defilement clinging to him, but with God's favour—a covenant of peace and an everlasting priesthood.

Atonement is an exchange involving the act of *being one with another*, so Phinehas, in making the decision to enter the curse, was taking the sin of the Israelites on himself. He was risking his life to stop the plague and save others from death; he was making atonement by carrying sin—not just the sin of the prince and the priestess, as well as the Israelites who had worshipped Baal-Peor, but his own sin in killing them. He knew the Law and undoubtedly expected to die.

Now many rabbinic commentators find God's approval of Phinehas' zeal in this passage highly problematic. Phinehas was clearly operating outside the law, he carried out his own sentence of capital punishment without due process, he was in fact guilty of murder and should have, in turn, been condemned to death. Other commentators, in an attempt to explain God's commendation, have devised justifying tales where they propose that Phinehas had rapidly convened a judicial court and was simply carrying out its orders.

But there is no hint of such legal proceedings in the text. Rather Phinehas seems to have calculated the cost of stopping the plague as being three more deaths: the prince Zimri, the priestess Cozbi and his own.

He foreshadows Jesus who went into the curse to save us from the plague of sin and death. Just as Phinehas understood execution would be the likely consequence of his zealotry, so did Jesus. His cleansing of the Temple prompted the authorities to decide He was too dangerous to live.

And yet Phinehas' action is not just a foreshadowing but also an echo of the past. Atonement is, among other things, a covering. And his atonement evokes the covering by Shem and Japheth of their father Noah as he lay in the tent.

Normally we associate the atonement of Jesus with His death but that's perhaps too restricted an understanding. I suspect John is showing us through these chiastic matchings that the atoning work of Jesus is not limited to His death but is to be found in each and every moment of His life. His healings of history are more than repairs of past national wounds—they are also bridges into atonement.

God awarded Phinehas a covenant of peace because he was willing to enter the curse to save the nation, just as Jesus was willing to enter the curse to save the world. Phinehas' swift action is a pale imitation of Jesus' long deliberate march towards death and it had a different outcome. Yet the motivation was similar. Their zeal sprang from the same source: loyalty to God.

Thus 'zeal' is not expressed in righteously administering punishment but rather in dispensing with the dark and unholy covenant that brings destruction. That, for us today, means our sin-plague has to be slain on the Cross. We don't have to use Phinehas as a role model to resolve the brokenness of our world—Jesus has already entered the curse on our behalf.

Although Jesus may call us to act as a covenant defender of another, we are not to be the Saviour, to—in old-fashioned parlance—be a 'sin-eater', 'disease-eater' or 'sympathy healer' and so deny the all-sufficiency of the atonement of Jesus. What we're effectively saying by such a belief is that Jesus needs help to atone for the sins of the world. We're acting as if His salvation is in some way defective without our input.

The covenant of peace is already available to us through Jesus.

Curiously, after receiving a covenant of peace, Phinehas was 'anointed for war'—and was sent out, not with sword or spear but with trumpets and holy objects. But then, our God-designed weapons are often mysterious:

> *The weapons of our warfare are not the weapons of the world. Instead, they have divine power to demolish strongholds.*
>
> 2 Corinthians 10:4^{BSB}

For God so loved the world that He gave His one and only Son,
that everyone who believes in Him shall not perish but have eternal life.
For God did not send His Son into the world to condemn the world,
but to save the world through Him.
Whoever believes in Him is not condemned,
but whoever does not believe has already been condemned,
because he has not believed in the name
of God's one and
only Son.

John 3:16-18
BSB

After this, knowing that everything had now been accomplished,
and to fulfill the Scripture, Jesus said, 'I am thirsty.'
A jar of sour wine was sitting there. So they soaked a sponge in the wine,
put it on a stalk of hyssop, and lifted it to His mouth.
When Jesus had received the sour wine,
He said, 'It is finished.' And bowing His head,
He yielded up
His spirit.

John 19:28-30 BSB

5.1 The Doorposts of Belief

> *For God so loved the world that He gave His one and only Son, that everyone who believes in Him shall not perish but have eternal life.*
>
> John 3:16[BSB]

ENTIRE BOOKS—SERIES OF BOOKS, in fact—could be written on this famous, well-beloved verse. So I am only going to focus on one aspect: what the chiasmus reveals.

The emphasis in this verse and those immediately following is threefold:

- God and His motivation for sending His Son
- God as Saviour, not as Judge
- Our response to the Son and the outcome of that response

God is looking for belief—saving belief that brings about obedience, not intellectual belief that makes no material difference to the way we run our lives. He's been looking for that since the pre-Flood days when the inclination of every human heart became evil, except for Noah who found grace in the eyes of the Lord. Noah turned out to have saving belief when he obeyed and built an ark.

Later, after the Flood, God looked for saving belief again—and found it in a man called Abram. God came to childless Abram in a vision and, taking him outside to look at the night sky, promised him his descendants would be as uncountable as the stars.

> *Abram believed the Lord, and it was credited to him as righteousness.*
>
> Genesis 15:6[ISV]

The word *believe* here is 'aman', *confirm, firm, stand firm, trust, support, establish, faithful, pillar, doorpost.*

It is that last possible meaning that John had in mind: *doorpost*. More specifically, he was thinking of a doorpost during the season of Passover—the very time when Jesus died. God instructed His people to use doorposts in ways we wouldn't normally consider:

- first, they were to be a memorial of God's words, and

- second, they were the place where, on Passover, the blood of the Lamb was to be applied with a stick of hyssop

The word for *doorpost* is 'mezuzah'. Over many centuries, the word came to refer to a container with a tiny scroll of Scripture inside it that was affixed to the doorpost near the hinge. Every time someone entered or exited a home or a city, they were directed by the presence of this mezuzah to remember God—to love Him and obey His commands.[98] And if they did, then God had promised they would prosper. There would be abundance.

The mezuzah was a symbol of saving belief through reciting and acting on the words of God. Just before the first Passover:

---

98 See Deuteronomy 11:18–24[ESV]

> *Moses called for all the elders of Israel and said to them, 'Go and take for yourselves lambs according to your families, and slay the Passover [lamb]. You shall take a bunch of hyssop and dip it in the blood which is in the basin, and apply some of the blood that is in the basin to the lintel and the two doorposts; and none of you shall go outside the door of his house until morning.'*
>
> Exodus 11:21–22^{NASB}

Just before another Passover:

> *Jesus knew that His mission was now finished, and to fulfil Scripture He said, 'I am thirsty.' A jar of sour wine was sitting there, so they soaked a sponge in it, put it on a hyssop branch, and held it up to His lips.*
>
> John 19:28–29^{NLT}

Before the first Passover, the blood of a lamb was applied to the doorpost using a hyssop branch. At the latter Passover, wine—symbolic of the new covenant in Jesus' blood—was applied to the bloodied Lamb of God using a hyssop branch. The imagery could hardly be more explicit: John is telling us, through his chiasmus, that Jesus *is* the Mezuzah of God. He is the Doorpost of Heaven, the Gate Pillar of Salvation.

Now John is later to recall one of Jesus' I AM statements as the 'Door of the Sheep', so this doorpost imagery isn't really as strange as it might initially seem.

The ordinary mezuzah at a doorway had a scroll portion with it. Just so, the Mezuzah of God had a scroll portion with Him, above His head. It read: *Jesus of Nazareth, the King of the Jews.*

This is the inscription that Jesus wants us to write on the gate of our heart. But, as John points out in his chiastic section, this is not merely about the kingship of the Jews, it's about the sovereignty of the world.

And that becomes clear in his fourth chapter where Jesus, once again, is thirsty. There He is travelling through Samaria when a conversation about water takes an interesting turn to focus on the elements involved in the anointing of a king.

5.2 The Thirst of the Living Water

From the beginning of John's gospel, lustral water has been a prominent theme. Lustral water is that set apart for a purification rite. The waters at Bethany-beyond-the-Jordan were used for a baptism of repentance, the water transformed into wine at the wedding feast came from six stone jars used for ceremonial washing and the waters of the new birth are infused by the Holy Spirit.

At the end of the third chapter, John the Baptiser is mentioned again, this time at Aenon near Salim, rather than in the old Brook Cherith at Bethany-beyond-the-Jordan. Once again, ceremonial washing and purification are mentioned—apparently in a discussion. In the next chapter, water from a special well, Jacob's Well at Sychar in Samaria, enables Jesus to begin a discussion about Living Water. Discussions about lustral water become important.

Living water, for the Jews, was water that flowed or bubbled up—not stagnant or still water. Living water wasn't quiet and brackish; it gushed and brought refreshment. Jesus hasn't yet called Himself the 'Living Water' in the fourth gospel but John has certainly paved the way for that revelation. But he also never lets us lose sight of the humanity of Jesus.

Jesus was thirsty. He was thirsty when He spoke to the woman at the well in Samaria; He was thirsty, agonisingly so, on the Cross.

Initially it seems that John is suggesting Jesus is quoting Scripture when He says, *'I am thirsty.'* However it seems highly unlikely that Jesus would be quoting the Canaanite general Sisera.[99]

There are several sentiments in the Hebrew Scriptures along the lines of 'my soul thirsts', particularly in the psalms, but the words, 'I am thirsty,' only occur in the story where Sisera is slain in the aftermath of a rout in battle caused by a flash-flood.

I am therefore inclined to believe that it is not the words of Jesus that John intends us to understand are the fulfilment of Scripture but rather what happens as a result of His words. Psalm 69, quoted in the second chapter of John's gospel, is referenced again:

> *They give me poison [gall] for food, they offer me sour wine for my thirst.*
>
> Psalm 69:21[NLT]

This provides a much better prophetic context: it's a psalm of David where he describes being surrounded by enemies and crying out continually for God's help in the face of humiliation, mockery and scorn.

Matthew tells us that the wine was mixed with gall, and Mark tells us that it was mixed with myrrh. This concoction was thought to deaden the pain of those being crucified. Matthew mentions that, after tasting it, Jesus refused to drink it. John doesn't record the refusal, simply that, after receiving some lifted to His mouth, He said, *'It is finished.'*

The Creator of all the waters of the earth, the Living Water who could Himself quench all thirsts, was thirsty. Perhaps, as the psalms said, it was more His soul that thirsted than His body.

---

99 Though, if He was, this is yet another pointer to Jesus' war with the Canaanite war goddess Anat.

5.3 The Bridegroom Speaks

'Tetelestai!'

'It is finished!'

The equivalent Aramaic word is 'kalot'. Brian Simmons points out that this climatic final saying of Jesus on the Cross has a much deeper meaning than simply a declaration that a task is accomplished, a mission is completed or a calling is fulfilled. 'Kalot' is the joyful cry of a bridegroom on his wedding night at the consummation of a marriage.[100]

The Greek cognate 'tetelestai' is not known to have been used within marriage festivities, but nevertheless it also meant *consummation*, not simply *finished*. Now, as mentioned previously, a Jewish wedding involved 'oil of joy'—*myrrh*—to celebrate the consummation of the marriage. The gospel of Mark mentions that myrrh was mingled with the sour wine that was lifted to Jesus' lips on a stick of hyssop. John tells us that, immediately after receiving this vinegary wine, Jesus called out, *'It is finished,'* and gave up His spirit.

---

100 Brian Simmons, *The Book of John: Eternal Love*, Broadstreet Publishing Group 2016

The 'oil of joy' traditionally associated with a new and wondrous moment of covenantal oneness was already there—even before Nicodemus, Joseph of Arimathea and the 'bridesmaids'[101] together created an aromatic mountain of spices. Who among them first realised that a royal wedding was in progress? Who first had the revelation that a splendid and sumptuous event was underway and that more myrrh was required? Who first understood that, with the flow of the blood and the water from Jesus' side, they'd watched the culmination of a nuptial ceremony as well as a birth? Who first had the incredible thought that they'd witnessed the union of the King of the Universe with His newly-created bride? Nicodemus is the most likely, but it could have been any of the witnesses.

It was Nicodemus, however, who gathered enough oil of joy to make a statement, to testify to the uniqueness of the occasion.

---

101 Mary Magdalene, Salome, Joanna, Mary the mother of James and Joseph, and at least one other woman. The various gospel accounts mention different women, though Mary Magdalene is usually given prominence. It would be very interesting if the final tally is five, suggesting that Jesus' parable about the wise and foolish bridesmaids was intended to be prophetic.

5.4 Everyone Who Believes

SALVATION, FOR THE GNOSTICS, came through the acquisition of esoteric knowledge and hidden mysteries. It was only available to a few, not to the many, and certainly not to the entire world. The widespread Jewish perception in the first century was that divine favour was shown through an individual's success or a family's prosperity—worldly wealth, position and power were indicators that God was handing out rewards that included salvation.

Consequently, the worldview of Jesus' followers was completely shattered when He said:

> 'It is easier for a camel to go through the eye of a needle than for a rich man to enter the kingdom of God.'
>
> Mark 10:25 NKJV

The disciples were so utterly astonished, they gasped:

> 'Who then can be saved?'
>
> Mark 10:26 NKJV

John tells us that Jesus explained to Nicodemus, an incredibly wealthy and powerful man, the simplicity of God's plan of salvation. It isn't about knowledge or understanding of the ways of heaven, it isn't about riches or authority, power or prestige. It's about something so straightforward that even a small child can grasp hold of it: trust in God—belief in Him sufficient to take His word at face value and obey it.

God loves the world—that's what Jesus told Nicodemus. And by repeating Christ's words, John is saying to his Gnostic opponents that creation is not evil; it's essentially good. It's been bent and warped by sin and God wants to restore it to His original design for it. But it's not the work of a malevolent demi-urge and it's not intrinsically foul. Even in its despoiled state, it shows the handiwork of God as beautiful and majestic. It points to what He is like: beautiful and majestic.

He loves it and its people—those He created to steward it. He has a plan to make all things new. And, in addition, He's decided to make it as easy as possible for humanity to participate and partner with Him in bringing this plan to fruition.

Just believe.

5.5 Everyone Who Doesn't Believe

> *For God did not send His Son into the world to condemn the world, but to save the world through Him. Whoever believes in Him is not condemned, but whoever does not believe has already been condemned, because he has not believed in the name of God's one and only Son.*
>
> John 3:17–18[BSB]

John 3:16 is almost certainly the most quoted verse in the gospels and epistles, and certainly a top contender for most beloved. I like it for an unusual reason: whenever I'm trying to remember the number of laws the Hebrews were required to obey, I think 3:16 and then reverse the numbers to get the correct answer, 613. It has a further claim to fame in my view—it must surely be in the running for the verse most often stripped of its context. The neighbouring verse is rarely mentioned:

> *Whoever does not believe has already been condemned, because he has not believed in the name of God's one and only Son.*
>
> John 3:18[BSB]

Yet this is a theme John the apostle returns to again. By the end of the chapter, John the Baptiser will testify:

> *Everyone who has faith in the Son has eternal life. But no one who rejects Him will ever share in that life, and God will be angry with them forever.*
>
> John 3:36^{CEV}

And later, Jesus will re-iterate and clarify what He has said to Nicodemus:

> *If anyone hears My words but does not keep them, I do not judge that person. For I did not come to judge the world, but to save the world. There is a judge for the one who rejects Me and does not accept My words; the very words I have spoken will condemn them at the last day.*
>
> John 12:47–48^{NIV}

In other words, we can't have it both ways. On the last day, we can't say: save us even though we don't believe in You or believe You can. We do not accept Your words that belief is necessary. So, since it is unnecessary, we don't need to believe in You or in Your words for You to save us. Even though You say we do. We know You better than You know Yourself. You are too loving to put any conditions on salvation.

In this argument, belief cannot be distinguished from unbelief—at least from the perspective of the outcome. Apparently neither belief nor unbelief matters in terms of salvation. Now God's sole condition essentially boils down to: you have to want to belong to Me. But that is irrelevant in this scheme of thought. Instead it's posited that God will override freewill; He's too loving not to. This ignores the reality that mature sacrificial love never abuses the agency of other people by countermanding their freewill decisions or taking coercive control of their self-will in determining their own destiny.

Ultimately this contradictory religious thought system suggests that, on the last day, we can rely on Jesus not to keep His word. That's a very peculiar understanding of trust. It says He's both trustworthy and untrustworthy at one and the same time.

God has thrown us a lifeline in the Cross of Jesus. But whether we take hold of the lifeline and believe in Him is our own choice. Because love does not deprive us of choice.

'And this is the verdict: The Light has come into the world, but men loved the darkness rather than the Light because their deeds were evil. Everyone who does evil hates the Light, and does not come into the Light for fear that his deeds will be exposed. But whoever practices the truth comes into the Light, so that it may be seen clearly that what he has done has been accomplished in God.'

After this, Jesus and His disciples went into the Judean countryside, where He spent some time with them and baptised.

Now John was also baptising in Aenon near Salim, because the water was plentiful there, and people kept coming to be baptised. (For John had not yet been thrown into prison.)

part

John 3:19-24 BSB

When the soldiers had crucified Jesus, they divided His garments into four parts, one for each soldier, with the tunic remaining. It was seamless, woven in one piece from top to bottom. So they said to one another, 'Let us not tear it. Instead, let us cast lots to see who will get it.' This was to fulfill the Scripture:

'They divided My garments among them, and cast lots for My clothing.'

So that is what the soldiers did.

Near the cross of Jesus stood His mother and her sister, as well as Mary the wife of Clopas and Mary Magdalene. When Jesus saw His mother and the disciple whom He loved standing nearby, He said to His mother, 'Woman, here is your son.' Then He said to the disciple, 'Here is your mother.' So from that hour, this disciple took her into his home.

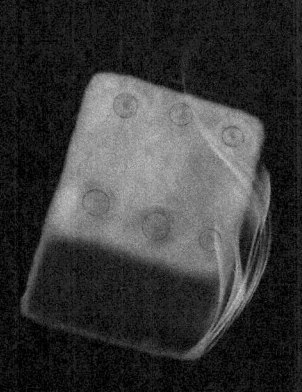
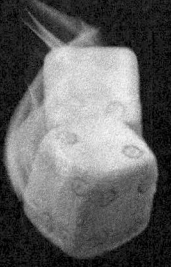
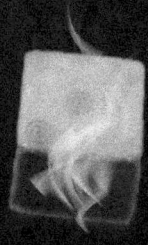

John 19:23-27 BSB

6.1 Light and Lots

And this is the verdict: the Light has come into the world, but men loved the darkness rather than the Light because their deeds were evil. Everyone who does evil hates the Light, and does not come into the Light for fear that his deeds will be exposed. But whoever practices the truth comes into the Light, so that it may be seen clearly that what he has done has been accomplished in God.

John 3:19–21^{BSB}

When the soldiers had crucified Jesus, they divided His garments into four parts, one for each soldier, with the tunic remaining. It was seamless, woven in one piece from top to bottom. So they said to one another, 'Let us not tear it. Instead, let us cast lots to see who will get it.' This was to fulfill the Scripture:

'They divided My garments among them, and cast lots for My clothing.'

So that is what the soldiers did.

John 19:23–24^{BSB}

JOHN NOW RETURNS TO A THEME that he first introduced in his opening chapter. There he spoke seven times of the Light—six times of light itself and once of en*light*ening—reminding us of the seven-branched candelabra, the menorah. Here he mentions light another five times, making twelve in all so far.

The condemnation that John has spoken of in the previous verses—the adverse judgment that falls on those who choose not to believe—is here spelled out in the Judge's verdict. The Judge's verdict makes it clear that people do not believe in Jesus because they would rather choose the covering of darkness than be clothed in His Light. The process will illuminate their evil deeds, and they cannot face the shame of that exposure.

Adam and Eve found the shame of their nakedness unbearable after their sin and, ever since, humanity has followed their lead in looking for suitable coverings. In general, a failure to process shame leads to the darkness of addiction or narcissism—two of the most destructive coverings we can throw over ourselves as substitutes for the Light.

This contrast between coverings—light and darkness—is not a mere metaphor. At least it wasn't for the Hebrews. There was a poetic relationship between *light*, 'owr', and *skin*, 'uwr'. Today's attitude towards wordplay in Scripture is to completely subordinate it to etymology, despite its profound interaction with prophecy.

John's gospel is an epic poem in the ancient prophetic style, matching ideas through chiasmus but also utilising poetic devices like rhyme, consonance and assonance. We're nearly a hundred verses into the gospel and there has yet to be a passage not mirrored at the back. There have been times when I've been ready to admit defeat when it came to discovering the thought behind a pair of parallels but, in the end, a check of all possible Hebrew words has always brought to light what he had in mind.

John was thinking in Hebrew while writing in Greek. It's that simple. His lyrical forms aren't always obvious on the surface. After all, poetry and humour are invariably the first casualties of translation. John's gospel is beautiful in Greek, but that loveliness is as nothing to its exquisite nature in Hebrew.

The costly garment that the soldiers were reluctant to rip up is a reminder of the 'ketonet', the covering made of skin, 'uwr',[102] that

God gave to Adam and Eve as they left Eden. The word 'ketonet' is used almost exclusively throughout Scripture for royal and priestly apparel.[103] The tunic worn by the high priest Aaron was a 'ketonet' and over it was placed the breastplate with its twelve gems and with the Urim and Thummim attached to it.

The Urim and Thummim are not described, so exactly what they looked like is unknown. Apart from the fact they were used to cast lots and make a judgment or deliver a verdict, they remain mysterious objects. Even the meaning of their names is unclear. Traditionally 'urim' has been thought to mean *lights*, since it's the plural of 'owr', *light, become light, flame* or *fire*. In recent years, however, a body of thought has arisen that suggests it is derived from a word for *curse*.

Yet John's chiastic match suggests the traditional understanding of *lights* was prevalent in the first century, since he mentions *light* five times along with *verdict, judgment, truth*, then combines those elements with *costly garment* and the *casting of lots* in his parallel.

All these evoke the high priest and the Urim he wore. Where the seven lights in the opening chapter suggested the menorah, now the cumulative total of twelve lights suggest the shining gems on the high priest's breastplate.[104]

---

102 This is the first time *skin* is mentioned in Scripture—Genesis 3:21.

103 The only exceptions are Joseph's coat-of-many-colours, which was a 'ketonet', and a rich robe worn by one of David's friends.

104 An alternative explanation for the five lights is that they point to the fifth night of Hanukkah, the festival of lights that is also known as the feast of dedication. This particular night always falls on the last day of the month, and thus on 'Yom Kippur Kattan', a so-called *small Day of Atonement*. Some communities keep this as a time of fasting and special prayer. If this is the allusion John was making, then he linked both episodes featuring the Baptiser with Yom Kippur: first with the main observance and then here with a minor one. For more on the fifth day of Hanukkah, see: chabad.org/therebbe/article_cdo/aid/2601667/jewish/5th-Night-of-Chanukah-28th-Day- of-Kislev-5740-1979.htm (accessed 23 August 2024)

6.2 Gambling Responsibly

John's allusions often point in two different directions at once: towards the Hebrew Scriptures as well towards cultural practices in the wider world. Sometimes those references to society at large are Greek in orientation, sometimes Roman, sometimes they are more in tune with ancient Canaanite observances that clearly still linger on in contemporary Judaic religious life.

So while on the one hand he's indicated that the Urim are a focus of his chiastic match, he's also given us other pointers to pursue. Gambling was illegal in the Roman empire, except during Saturnalia,[105] the darkest time of year—during the week leading up to the winter solstice in December. Originally seven days of riotous holiday, Caesar Augustus reduced it to three days and later Caligula increased that to five. Regardless of imperial decree, it seems to have been celebrated for a week. During this time, the usual conventions of society were overturned—masters served slaves, slaves did not have to work, men wore colourful casual clothes instead of the formal toga. It was a time of merriment

---

105 This rule applied to men. For women it was still illegal, except during the days of Bona Dea, *good goddess*, generally celebrated in May. The identity of the 'good goddess' is not known since her festivities were forbidden to men—and it was men who left the written records of ancient Rome.

and feasting where a Lord of Misrule was appointed to command others to perform outrageous actions.[106]

On the last day of the festival, 'sigillaria'—pottery or wax figurines—were given as gifts. So were 'cerei', *wax candles*, as a reminder of an old prophecy given to the earliest inhabitants of Latium, the region around Rome. The Latin people were directed by this oracle to send heads to Hades, ruler of the underworld, and 'phota' to the elder-god Saturn. The word 'phota' was originally taken to be *man* and thus it seems the people initially practised human sacrifice. However, according to ancient tradition, the strongman Hercules advised using candles instead of human heads because 'phos' means *light* and, consequently, with a slight change in accent, 'phota' means *light* as well as *man*.[107] Thus the candles became a substitute offering to Saturn for the *light of life*.[108]

The Light who is a man: is this not Jesus? John used 'phos' eleven of the twelve times he described Jesus in his first three chapters. The other time he used 'photizei', *to give light, to enlighten, to shine, to brighten*.

The Light who is a man, sacrificed during the darkest of times—a man being sent to hell, Hades, at a skull-shaped hill, a man acknowledged as a king and yet treated as a slave, a man laughed at and mocked—there's enough spiritual atmosphere here to evoke Saturnalia or its Greek equivalent, Kronia.[109] So perhaps, responsive to the overall ambience, the Roman soldiers felt free to ignore the law and gamble anyway. Or perhaps they simply took advantage of the darkness of the eclipse.

---

106 penelope.uchicago.edu/~grout/encyclopaedia_romana/calendar/saturnalia.html (accessed 18 November 2023)

107 britannica.com/topic/Saturnalia-Roman-festival (accessed 18 November 2023)

108 en.wikipedia.org/wiki/Saturnalia (accessed 18 November 2023)

109 en.wikipedia.org/wiki/Kronia (accessed 18 November 2023)

Kronia, held in late July or early August, was named for Kronos, originally an agricultural deity, who was often identified with Khronos, Father Time.

Here John foreshadows two major chiastic episodes later in his gospel: the story of the man born blind who is healed by the 'Light of the World' in parallel with Lazarus brought back to experience the light of life by the 'Resurrection and the Life'. In both these cases we see Jesus challenging the powers of darkness—for Sheol, *hell*, in the Hebrew conception was a place of shrouded mist where it was impossible to see properly.

Jesus had promised that the Gates of Hades would not prevail against His church. And through His death and then resurrection He proves that the lords of the underworld, in whatever pantheon—Roman, Greek, Egyptian, Canaanite—have been taken on at their own game and bested. It isn't simply that Jesus whopped them; He played by their house rules—the ones designed to ensure they never lost—and triumphed anyway.

6.3 Light of Life

The Hebrew word for *light*, 'owr', has a variant form, 'owrah', meaning *herb, luminary, light of life*. Perhaps there's a thought behind this that green plants are 'light encapsulated'—after all, without photosynthesis, they don't grow. Without water, they don't grow either. This fusion of light and water powers the cycle of life in the natural world. And, as in the natural, so in the spiritual.

Light is mentioned five times in the discourse between Nicodemus and Jesus. It seems a little strange. What do five lights represent? Not the menorah, nor the Festival of Lights. The five days of Saturnalia at the time John was writing? That hardly seems likely.

It seems to me that John was attempting to match 'five lights' with 'five garments': the Roman soldiers divided the clothing of Jesus into four shares but, on faced with the beautiful seamless tunic, they were unwilling to ruin it. This suggests there were five pieces of apparel. This match between *light* and *garment* directs us back to aspects of the story of Adam and Eve.

The reversal of the sin in Eden is John's theme throughout his record of the crucifixion and resurrection: he's working up to the moment when water and blood-spirit flow from the pierced side of the Second Adam and the new Eve is birthed. Then he goes beyond to tell of an incident where a representative of humanity comes looking for God in a garden, just as once God came looking for humanity in a garden.

Ancient cultures generally thought of clothing as an overskin or a second skin—this was, after all, very natural since in the earliest time, clothing was mainly animal skins. When Adam and Eve are exiled from Eden, their 'ketonet' is made of animal skin.

Now one highly disputed theory regarding Adam and Eve suggests they were originally clothed in light, just as God is:

> *The Lord wraps Himself in light as with a garment.*
>
> Psalm 104:2^{NIV}

This covering of *light*, 'owr', was lost when they sinned and so God gave them a covering of *skin*, 'uwr'. According to this theory, they only realised they were naked when their skin of *light*, 'owr', simply vanished. This is why they felt shame and scrabbled to cover themselves in leaves from 'owrah'.

Now, despite the controversial nature of this belief, I think that John's chiastic parallel indicates he understands it to be true. He's explicitly linked *clothing* to *light* and, for his readers who know of the eclipse mentioned in Luke's gospel, he subtly connected nakedness to darkness.

Jesus was naked on the cross, deprived of His clothing. John has led us to understand that this means He was deprived of His wrapping of light. Yet of course this must be the case since, as the Second Adam, He is in the process of reversing the loss of covering for mankind. As Adam was once covered in light, so those who believe will be covered by the Light.

He is the Light of Life and He will also see the light of life—as prophesied by Isaiah in his account of the Suffering Servant:

He was pierced for our transgressions, He was crushed for our iniquities; the punishment that brought us peace was on Him, and by His wounds we are healed...

After He has suffered, He will see the light of life and be satisfied; by His knowledge, My righteous servant will justify many, and He will bear their iniquities.

Isaiah 53:5;11^{NIV}

Isaiah 53:5;11 [NIV]

John's chiasmus evokes beautiful imagery in the vision recorded in Revelation of the New Eve:

'a woman clothed in the sun.'

Revelation 12:1 [NIV]

A return to the Light is an acceptance of the atonement of Jesus.

6.4 MOTHER AND SON

After this, Jesus and His disciples went into the Judean countryside, where He spent some time with them and baptised.

Now John was also baptising at Aenon near Salim, because the water was plentiful there, and people kept coming to be baptised. (For John had not yet been thrown into prison.)

John 3:22–24^{BSB}

Now there stood by the cross of Jesus His mother, and His mother's sister, Mary the wife of Clopas, and Mary Magdalene. When Jesus therefore saw His mother, and the disciple whom He loved standing by, He said to His mother, 'Woman, behold your son!' Then He said to the disciple, 'Behold your mother!' And from that hour that disciple took her to his own home.

John 19:25–27^{NKJV}

THIS ENTIRE SERIES OF BOOKS STARTED because I forgot a single piece of information. Somewhere I'd read that John the apostle had indicated he was the unnamed 'beloved disciple' because he'd positioned this description so that it formed a chiastic placement with John the Baptiser. *Somewhere.* I couldn't remember where. I decided to google it. I quickly found lots of small lists with parallel themes in John's gospel and thought I should combine them. Once I'd got the idea of how it worked, I was able to find another half dozen or so chiastic formations myself. So I decided to write a very small booklet. But as soon as I was systematic in my approach—looking at the very first and very last verses—I realised the chiasmus was so intense, so all-pervading, that I was looking at an epic poem. By the time I'd matched up all of the first and last chapters, eventually solving the riddle of why a loose sandal is like 153 fish, my curiosity was hooked. My mother always said that, if she'd been born in a different era, she'd have liked to have been a detective—and I feel that, in the best way possible, I'm fulfilling that calling on her life.

This investigation all started over a correspondence of names involving John the apostle and John the Baptiser. Now, actually I'd remembered the details somewhat incorrectly. It was Richard Bauckham who made the statement about the chiasmus but it was his belief that it referred to a disciple who is separate from the son of Zebedee. Bauckham called him 'John the elder'. Regardless, it's about someone named John.

Here in the third and third-last chapter we encounter the same formation as in the first and last chapters. The anonymous 'beloved disciple' is paralleled with John the Baptiser. We have confirmation that the 'beloved disciple' is indeed John.

Both events—the death of Jesus on the Cross and, much earlier, His disciples baptising—happen in the Judean countryside. Jesus was taken outside Jerusalem, beyond the walls, to be crucified.

> *Jesus suffered and died outside the city gates to make His people holy by means of His own blood. So let us go out to Him, outside the camp, and bear the disgrace He bore.*
>
> Hebrews 13:12–13[NLT]

Baptism is a symbol of repentance; it signifies a change of mind and an intention to change our life and behaviour. Yet it is the blood of Jesus shed on the Cross, and now speaking on our behalf in heaven, that empowers us to achieve our intentions as proclaimed through the symbol of baptism.

Baptism is also a sign of being brought into the family of God, of being granted a place in the Lord's household. That's the story John presents us with in the parallel—a woman being granted a place in a man's family and household, even though they are not related.

Although most translations say, *'When Jesus therefore saw His mother, and the disciple whom He loved,'* in fact, the text says THE *mother*, not *His* mother. Through this small grammatical point, John directs our attention to Eve, *the mother of all living*. John, about to reveal the nature of the 'birth from above' Nicodemus had questioned, is building towards the imminent unveiling of the Bridegroom, the second Adam, along with the birth of the Bride, the new Eve. Here, on Golgotha, the waters broke and the birth pangs for the church began—Christ as the Head, with the disciples—the three Marys, Salome, Joanna, Nicodemus, Joseph of Arimathea, John himself and perhaps others—as the Body.

Still this action of Jesus in handing over care of His mother to John seems strange in many ways. Why did He make this declaration? What about His brothers—James, Joses, Simon and Jude? Why didn't He tell John to escort her to one of them to ensure she was safe?

Perhaps, in addition to the message about baptism, John told his readers this story to explain his relationship with Mary. Tradition suggests that, when he went to Ephesus, he took her with him. It would have been an unusual domestic set-up. A man taking care of an older woman who is not part of his own biological family or one of his in-laws would have invited comment. Perhaps even salacious comment. So this explanation covers the whys and wherefores of the relationship. Except that it still leaves that gaping hole of a question—what about James, Joses, Simon and

Jude? And what about the sisters of Jesus and their husbands?

If Joseph had died, then Mary should have been taken care of by Jesus. When He began His itinerant ministry, He apparently left her in the care of His brothers. For some reason, Jesus concluded they were not up to this role. Yet, within a few short years, they'd stepped up to leading positions in the early church.

Now we know, from John's artfully constructed second and second-last chapters, that there was a rift in the family going at least as far back as the time of the Cana wedding.[110] The brothers of Jesus were, according to the subtle clues provided by John, concerned about inheritance. They were jealous and insecure. The estrangement continued and was still current at the time of Jesus' death—as evidenced by His direction to Mary Magdalene in the garden to tell His brothers and sisters the news of His resurrection. They, clearly, from this instruction are not with the disciples. Moreover it's implied that the disciples would not think to inform them.[111]

Still, at some point, James and Jude do a complete turnaround and become ardent followers of Jesus. Perhaps the others do as well. James steps up to become the leader of the early church in

---

110 See Anne Hamilton, *The Summoning of Time: John 2 and 20* for more details.

111 Most commentators think that when Jesus directs the Magdalene to tell His brothers—and, it should be noted, *sisters* too, since 'adelphos', *from the same womb*, covers both—He is changing the status of His disciples from followers to family. True as that may be in the wider scheme of things, I believe Jesus is sending the Magdalene to his natural kin, the brothers and sisters He grew up with. He doesn't need to send her to the disciples—she's already told them and, besides that, Peter and John have seen the empty tomb. Their testimony will count for far more than that of a woman. But the sons and daughters of Joseph of Nazareth need to know too. Jesus shows His care for them in this moment. If His disciples were afraid of the Jews, how much more so would His own family have been?

Jerusalem, and both he and Jude wrote epistles that managed to survive and make it into the canon of Scripture.

Apart from His mother, the only other relative of Jesus at the Cross was His aunt—His mother's sister. Some translations indicate she was Mary, the wife of Clopas, and some leave her unnamed and suggest that Mary, the wife of Clopas, was a separate woman. Early church tradition points to 'sister' as 'sister-in-law'[112] and that Clopas was actually Joseph's brother. Clopas and Mary were the uncle and aunt of Jesus. Clopas is also regarded as the same person as Cleopas, mentioned in Luke's gospel as one of the two disciples walking to Emmaus.[113] We're not talking blood relatives here. In fact, the closest relation by blood—again apart from His mother—is mentioned in the chiastic section: John the Baptiser.

Those brothers who grew up with Jesus are absent. Lest we judge them too harshly, I sometimes wonder if I'd be too much different. We might think they should have trusted their mother when she spoke of the appearance of the angel Gabriel to announce the birth of Jesus. And we might think they'd have listened to their father when he verified Mary's story. And perhaps they did. The trouble with believing their parents is that the only grid reference they'd have for such an event was the angel who appeared to Manaoh and his wife to announce the birth of Samson. Now Samson, when he got to marrying age, threw over all his Nazarite upbringing, played verbal and cultural games with the Philistines and provoked them to retaliatory violence. He took the gates ('shaar') of Gaza, *strength*, and the men of Gaza took his hair ('shaar') and, with it, his strength. Ultimately, Samson brought the house down—literally—on himself and a jeering crowd.

---

112 The same word was used for both sister and sister-in-law in the first century.
113 See Anne Hamilton, *The Summoning of Time: John 2 and 20 or Silk Shadows, Rings of Gold: Jesus and the Healing of History 03*, Armour Books 2020

Now I can imagine Jesus' brothers hearing of His parables and His sparring with the scribes and Pharisees, and wondering not *if*, but *when*, He's going to throw over all His Nazarene upbringing and it's all going to turn sour as it did for Samson. As rumours of death threats filtered back to them, surely it would have occurred to them it was all going to end very, very badly at the hands of foreign oppressors, just as it did for Samson. Their assertion that Jesus was crazy might well have been their attempt to safeguard Him. The fact that they were jealous and insecure doesn't mean to say that they wouldn't have done their utmost to protect Him.

6.5 Reuben's Mantle

Reuben was the firstborn son of Jacob. Under normal circumstances he was entitled to inherit a double blessing. That birthright was both a privilege and an immense responsibility. It was bestowed for a practical reason: the firstborn, on the death of his father, was expected to assume the role of the patriarchal provider and care for all the widows and orphans in the family.

Reuben's portion was, however, given to Judah. On his deathbed, Jacob bypassed his eldest in favour of his fourth-born son with the proclamation:

> *Reuben, you are my firstborn, my might, and the firstfruits of my strength, preeminent in dignity and preeminent in power. Unstable as water, you shall not have preeminence, because you went up to your father's bed; then you defiled it—he went up to my couch!*
>
> Genesis 49:3–4[ESV]

Here, Jacob alluded to Reuben's intimate relationship with Bilhah, Reuben's step-mother and, Jacob's third wife. The phrase *'unstable as water'* has a subtle innuendo of sexual turbulence.

Reuben's role in Scripture is comparatively small and the details of his life are sparse. As a boy, he found some mandrakes in a field and gave them to his mother—the aphrodisiac nature of the gift perhaps foreshadowed the lusts of later years.

He played a significant part in Joseph's saga, attempting to save him from the murderous jealousy of nine other brothers. He would have succeeded too, had not the nine removed Joseph from the pit and sold him into slavery before Reuben's rescue could be effected.

Now, just as Reuben went to the pit and found it empty, so in a later era, Peter and John would go to the tomb of Jesus and find it empty. Peter, as noted in *The Elijah Tapestry*, was given Elijah's mantle by Jesus. John, it would appear, was gifted Reuben's mantle.

Now a mantle is not to repeat the works of those who held it previously. It is to finish the assignment that remains incomplete and also to mend the mistakes and heal the history of those who have worn it in the past.

Reuben's mantle was meant to carry inestimable honour: the birthright and double blessing of the firstborn. The prophecy of gushing water needed to be fulfilled in purity and honour, devoid of sexual transgression. The new bearer, in being given by Jesus a mantle restored to its original design, would be required to take on the responsibility of repairing the consequences of sexual sin towards a mother figure and also carry out the normal assignment of the firstborn by caring for the bereaved in the family—the widows and orphans.

John, the one whose name is inextricably associated with water and the only one of the Twelve to witness the death of Jesus and the new birth in water and in Spirit, is the firstborn of their company. He is the Reuben of the new brotherhood. He is tasked with caring for the family and, in particular, for Jesus' own widowed mother. Whatever His practical reasons for overlooking the sons and sons-in-law of his foster-father Joseph in the matter of caring for Mary, Jesus also had His spiritual reasons. The appointed hour for handing on the renewed mantle of Reuben had come.

And like the original Reuben, whose name means *behold, a son*, the apostle John is proclaimed a son and protector when Jesus says of him to His mother Mary, '*Behold, your son.*'

The assembly of Christians at Ephesus, and perhaps even beyond, apparently realised that John was a Reuben figure. As the end of the first century approached, he was the elder statesman of the church, the last of the Twelve left alive, the only remaining member of the original group that Jesus called to follow Him. Assuming that the church did indeed understand John as the firstborn, since he was present at the crucifixion and thus at the new birth, and assuming that they did indeed see him as the inheritor of Reuben's mantle, then the rumour that John would not die makes sense. It is one way of interpreting the prophetic blessing of Moses:

> *May Reuben live and not die, nor may his people be few.*
>
> Deuteronomy 33:6[NASB]

In Aramaic, the language of first century Jewish people, this would have been rendered: 'Reuben shall live and not die…'[114]

Although it refers to the continuity of the tribe, it's ripe for imaginative re-interpretation. No wonder John was at pains to set the record straight in the final words of his gospel. Firstborn among the apostles he might have been and inheritor of Reuben's mantle too, but Jesus had made no explicit promises that he would not see death.

---

[114] See: Jeremy Chance Springfield, randomgroovybiblefacts.com/a_second_death.html (accessed 26 August 2024)

Reuben did not receive the mantle of his father, Jacob. The birthright and blessing of the firstborn bypassed him, as we've seen, in favour of Judah and, to a lesser extent, Joseph. Jacob's mantle, in its own right, appears to have been granted to Nathanael. This is indicated in John's first chapter where the comments of Jesus about Nathanael are replete with symbols of Jacob:

> 'Behold, an Israelite indeed, in whom is no guile!'
>
> John 1:47^{KJV}

This play on words and on the identity of Jacob who was renamed Israel can be re-stated: 'Here is a man of Israel in whom there is no Jacob.' It is confirmed by the reference to Jacob's vision of the angels ascending and descending on a 'sullam'.

The mantle of Jacob was stained by deceit, dispossession, theft of blessing and birthright, blatant favouritism and bias amongst his children, failure to protect his daughter and projecting blame onto his sons for his own lack of parenting. The mantle needed to pass to a man of superlative integrity in order to have a chance of repair.

In addition, of course, to the flaws just mentioned, Jacob was—like so many others after him—completely neglectful when it came to sharing the knowledge of the God of his fathers. The idea of being a 'blessing to all nations' and a 'light to the Gentiles' never translated into speaking about God to those outside the tribal brotherhood—an oversight or blind spot that continued on to Joseph and then down, as noted throughout this series, as far as the prophets Elijah, Elisha, Jonah and beyond. Jacob the patriarch apparently did not even share his family's experiential revelation of El Shaddai with his cousins, the sons of Laban, in the land of Paddan-Aram.

In this, at least, Nathanael brought healing to history. The early records of Christianity indicate he spread the gospel through

Arabia and Armenia, serving with his fellow-apostle Jude Thaddeus for a time.[115] Jude had focussed on Edessa, the capital of Armenian Mesopotamia—a town just a short distance from the old cross-roads of Harran in Paddan-Aram. Nathanael went back to the very same locality Abraham had left with Sarah and his nephew Lot, where Eleazar had found a wife for his master's son Isaac, and where Jacob had fled and where he'd found his brides, Rachel and Leah. This was the ancient homeland of the progenitor of all the Hebrews.

Nathanael and Jude were so successful in their evangelisation efforts that, at the beginning of the fourth century, the king of Edessa proclaimed the entire territory to be a Christian nation.

---

115   See: Elva Schroeder, *Whatever Happened to the Twelve Apostles?*, Even Before Publishing 2010

6.6 The Tree of Weeping

> *Near the cross of Jesus stood His mother and her sister, as well as Mary the wife of Clopas and Mary Magdalene.*
>
> John 19:25[BSB]

John confirms the detail mentioned in both the gospel of Matthew and that of Mark—the Magdalene was present at the crucifixion. Matthew adds a seemingly minor point to his description of the scene: she sat with another Mary.

> *Mary Magdalene and the other Mary were there, sitting opposite the tomb.*
>
> Matthew 27:61[ESV]

Such a tiny detail seems inconsequential, yet once we become attuned to the nature of the war Jesus is conducting against the powers, it's another clue to enable us to identify the role of the Magdalene in the final battle. She is the one who stands in the light to oppose her dark counterpoint Anat—and she is given Joseph's mantle to do so. She is called to finish Joseph's unfinished task: to undo the dispossession he inflicted on the world. For it was not only Egypt that suffered through Joseph's decrees—in the fullness of time, his own people reaped what he had sown.

Down the ages, others had come to inherit Joseph's mantle. Joshua and Ahab were two completely contrasting leaders who each bore that mantle in their own era and who used it in completely different ways. Amongst the women who carried on the mantle and its mandate for a return of inheritance was Deborah, the prophet and war-leader.

The Magdalene sat near the tomb in the vicinity of the Cross. The image of a woman warrior judge sitting beneath a tree was a significant one in Israelite history.[116] This is a picture of Deborah who delivered her verdicts from the Palm of Deborah between Bethel and Ramah. It's possible that Ramah near Bethel in later times became known as Arimathea.[117] This is the same locality that the original Deborah was buried beneath 'the tree of weeping'.

The first Deborah was the nurse of Rebekah. She appears out of nowhere in Genesis; nothing is recorded of her life—just that she died and was buried near Bethel. It's one of those strange inclusions in Scripture. We don't learn any aspects of Rebekah's death but we do get a sudden detail about a figure we've never been previously introduced to in the narrative. Trees are important in the stories of both Deborahs. So they must be important in the account of the new Deborah: Mary the Magdalene.

---

116 By the time John's gospel was written he would have known that the Romans had turned the ancient iconography of the warrior woman judge on its head. They issued coins after the conquering of Jerusalem, stamped with the words 'Iudea capta', *Judea captive*, and with the image of a woman who represented the defeated nation, sitting and mourning under a palm tree alongside the armour of the conquered Jews. See: library.biblicalarchaeology.org/wp-content/uploads/2023/11/Warrior-Women-BAR-Winter-2023.pdf (accessed 1 February 2024)

117 It is widely thought that Arimathea is to be identified as Ramathaim-Zophim, the birthplace of Samuel. It is also thought that Ramathaim-Zophim might simply be Ramah of the Zuphites (to distinguish it from any other Ramah, of which there were many, since it simply means *height* or *high place*) and that it was locally known as Ramah.

The Cross is the ultimate 'tree of weeping'. It was there that Jesus said to His mother, *'Woman, behold your son,'*[118] placing her in the care of John. The Aramaic word for *woman* is 'anath'—the Greek form of the goddess Anat's name. Throughout the scene at the Cross, there are subtle reminders of Deborah's victory over the cosmic rulers of appointed time, possession and dispossession, destiny and calling.

There might be a birth and a wedding in progress, but there's also a war.

---

118   John 19:26[NKJV]

6.7 Aenon near Salim

Neither Aenon nor Salim are known outside of John's gospel. In the fourth century, the early Christian chronicler Eusebius suggested Aenon was situated near Salumias about twelve kilometres south of Beit She'an. Further south is another possible location—the Tirzah stream where there are many springs. A place called 'Ainun exists about five kilometres from the springs.[119]

Salumias at the junction of the Jordan and Jezreel valleys is a very attractive solution since it would have been almost directly opposite the mouth of the stream flowing out from the Wadi al-Yabis. The stream in this wadi is believed to be the Brook Cherith,

---

119 This site is certainly not out of contention because John 4 may contain very subtle allusions to Tirzah.

120 Bethabara (also called Al-Maghtas) near Jericho is often cited as a possible locality for Bethany-beyond-the-Jordan. I prefer the identification with the Brook Cherith in the north because of its unique link to Elijah. Certainly the Jordan crossing near Jericho is also linked to Elijah, but it has other associations as well including the original passage into the Promised Land. Thus Bethabara is not a unique identifier back to Elijah. In addition, John the apostle mentions that Jesus and His disciples went out into the Judean countryside where they were baptising. This suggests they were active much closer to Jerusalem than John the Baptiser was. Although there is implied rivalry between the two sets of disciples, I believe Jesus would not only *do* the right thing but be *seen to be doing* the right thing. Thus it's my view that the disciples of Jesus performed baptisms in Judea, while John did so first in the territory that was once Gilead, then later in Galilee.

famed as Elijah's hideout during the time he was fed by ravens. The location of Bethany-beyond-the-Jordan, where John was first baptising, is disputed[120] but I believe it was here, in the old Brook Cherith in the ancient territory of Gilead. This would tie John the Baptiser's ministry to Elijah from the very start. It would also mean that, when John moved from one bank of the Jordan to the other, he wasn't going very far.

Now for the sake of completeness and also because the faintest of hints point in this direction, I'd like to suggest another possibility. If, instead of going twelve kilometres south from Beit She'an, we go the same distance west-north-west, we'd come to the Spring of Harod where Gideon famously split his fighting force according to how the men drank water. 'Aenon' simply means *spring* or *fountain* and this watering place had been renowned in Israelite history. It is the 'spring in Jezreel' where Saul and Jonathan camped before their defeat by the Philistines on nearby Mount Gilboa. Prior to the battle, the Philistines had camped close by at Shunem, later to be known as Sulam. So could 'Aenon near Salim' refer to the famous spring near Sulam?

It's worth considering because the spring was, all through antiquity, on the Via Maris, *the Way of the Sea*, a major trade route through the Middle East from Egypt to Damascus and then on to the Euphrates. That was why Pharaoh Necho was heading up this road—he was en route to the Euphrates and simply wanted through-passage. He asked Josiah not to come against him, but Josiah wasn't willing to listen. It was near this site that Josiah received his mortal wound.

Just as significant in all these considerations is the fact that Sulam was right next door to the village of Nain.

The spring would have been the water source for Naboth's vineyard—the fertile plot of ground coveted by King Ahab for a vegetable garden. Ahab's wife Jezebel obtained the land for him through false accusation and murder, thereby dispossessing an entire family of their inheritance. Since a major theme of John's gospel is the return of inheritance and the overturning of dispossession, then such an allusion would fit well at this point. Particularly since the story of Ahab falls into the same pattern as the story of Joseph. They were both rulers who had:

- to deal with drought and famine
- fathers-in-law who were priests of a sun-god[121]
- exempted the priests from the imposed famine restrictions
- wives who were named for Canaanite deities
- dispossessed others of their land
- initiated significant building projects

The famine during Ahab's time was half as long as Joseph's. He kept a table where 850 prophets were wined and dined. His wife Jezebel was named for Baal-Hadad and his daughter Athaliah was named for Baal's sister, Anat, as well as Yahweh.[122] Joseph's wife Asenath was also named for Anat and he himself was renamed by Pharaoh with one of Anat's titles. Joseph also dispossessed the Egyptians of their land and made no provision for its return. He was eventually buried in Shechem, the original capital of Ahab's kingdom in Samaria.

It appears from these parallels that Ahab inherited Joseph's mantle. It had been borne by Deborah during the period of the Judges and, as far as the Scriptural record relates, she used it wisely. Her major victory, by the way, occurred in the Valley of Jezreel, close

---

121 Generally he is called a priest of Astarte, but occasionally, as for example here— studylight.org/commentaries/eng/cpc/ezekiel-28.html (accessed 23 July 2024) —he is considered the representative of the Phoenician sun-deity.
122 This combination is not unusual. The Jews who lived in Egypt five centuries before Christ syncretised Anat and Yahweh as Anat-Yahu.

to all the locations mentioned in this section. Ahab seems to have been called to be the Joseph of his day, to build storehouses and granaries, not a palace of pearl. He was meant to feed the people in time of drought and famine, just as Joseph did, but also to repair the mistakes his predecessor had made. Instead, he repeated them and was involved with the dispossession of others.

The vegetable garden by the spring of Jezreel—Gideon's pool, the fountain of Harod—had been the vineyard of Naboth's family. Naboth's sons were killed as well, so there was no possibility the family could claim their inheritance back.

Now the reason I think there's a strong possibility John the apostle may be referring to this historical background when he mentioned Aenon is because he's about to bring up dispossession once again. The reference to Aenon is the prelude to the story of John the Baptiser saying that Jesus is not usurping him, not dispossessing him, not taking advantage of him, not stealing from him nor depriving him of anything.

In addition, the death of sons—not just Naboth's but Ahab's too,[123] since they are disposed of on this land—should remind us of the miracle at Nain. Now it's impossible to know who Jesus first raised from the dead. It could have been the daughter of Jairus or the son of the widow at Nain. It was very unlikely to have been Lazarus, since that happened just a few months, perhaps even a few weeks, before the Passover when Jesus died. Regardless of who was first, these three raisings double the previous combined total for all of history:

- the raising of the son of the widow of Zarephath by Elijah
- the raising of the son of the woman of Shunem (later Sulam) by Elisha

---

123   Also his grandsons.

- the raising of the dead man whose body touched Elisha's bones when he was thrown in Elisha's tomb just as a Moabite raiding party appeared

Personally I suspect that the first raising by Jesus has to have been the son of the widow from Nain. Its proximity to Shunem, just over the Hill of Moreh, with its historic link to Elisha would have immediately established Jesus as the new Elisha—and therefore the successor to John the Baptiser. The raising of the widow's son legitimised Jesus as one who could wear Elijah's mantle after Elisha, and also after John the Baptiser.

So, in summary: although I think Aenon is most likely to be in the Jordan Valley opposite Wadi al-Yabis for purely practical reasons, I'm really tempted for spiritual and historic considerations to think it might have been Gideon's pool, Ein Harod, at Jezreel. Being in Galilee on such a major highway, it would have given John the Baptiser access to an increasingly Gentile audience—and that, as outlined in *The Elijah Tapestry*, is a portion of the unfinished task of anyone who is granted Elijah's mantle.

Furthermore, when it comes to spiritual and historic reasons, Jesus was always mending the past. It would be unlike the Holy Spirit to miss an opportunity to direct John to a place where repentance for historic wrongs was so profoundly needed.

Then a dispute arose between John's disciples and a certain Jew over the issue of ceremonial washing. So John's disciples came to him and said, 'Look, Rabbi, the One who was with you beyond the Jordan, the One you testified about—He is baptising, and everyone is going to Him.'

John replied, 'A man can receive only what is given him from heaven. You yourselves can testify that I said, "I am not the Christ, but am sent ahead of Him." The bride belongs to the bridegroom. The friend of the bridegroom stands and listens for him, and is overjoyed to hear the bridegroom's voice. That joy is mine, and it is now complete. He must increase; I must decrease.'

Part

John 3:25-30

BSB

Then Pilate handed Jesus over to be crucified, and the soldiers took Him away.
Carrying His own cross, He went out to The Place of the Skull,
which in Hebrew is called Golgotha. There they crucified Him,
and with Him two others, one on each side, with Jesus in the middle.

Pilate also had a notice posted on the cross. It read:

JESUS OF NAZARETH, THE KING OF THE JEWS.

Many of the Jews read this sign, because the place where Jesus was crucified
was near the city, and it was written in Hebrew, Latin, and Greek.
So the chief priests of the Jews said to Pilate, 'Do not write,
"The King of the Jews," but only that He said,
"I am the King of the Jews."'

Pilate answered,
'What I have written,
I have written.'

Seven

John 19:16-22
BSB

7.1 A Dispute about Ceremonial Washing

Then a dispute arose between John's disciples and a certain Jew over the issue of ceremonial washing.

So John's disciples came to him and said, 'Look, Rabbi, the One who was with you beyond the Jordan, the One you testified about—He is baptising, and everyone is going to Him.'

John 3:25–26[BSB]

Pilate also had a notice posted on the cross. It read:

JESUS OF NAZARETH,
THE KING OF THE JEWS.

Many of the Jews read this sign, because the place where Jesus was crucified was near the city, and it was written in Hebrew, Latin, and Greek. So the chief priests of the Jews said to Pilate, 'Do not write, THE KING OF THE JEWS, *but only that He said, "I am the King of the Jews."'*

Pilate answered, 'What I have written, I have written.'

John 19:19–22[BSB]

Both these situations involve disputes between the Jewish leaders and another party over ceremonial washing. John does not go into details about the issue between 'a certain Jew' and the Baptiser's disciples. He simply pairs this dispute with that of Pilate over the claims of Jesus. Some commentators think the 'certain Jew' was Nicodemus but I doubt that. As for the lack of details, perhaps it's unnecessary to mention them since the real debate is obviously one of authority.

Just as the leaders were questioning Pilate's authority to write what he did, so one of them was questioning the Baptiser's authority to wash as he did. Although Pilate is not mentioned in this gospel as ceremonially washing his hands and declaring himself innocent of the blood of Jesus, the apostle's readers would have picked up just these nuances from Matthew's gospel.

Neither the Baptiser nor Pilate was going to 'repent' of their behaviour. They weren't changing their minds or rectifying anything they'd done. They stood by their actions. Both testified to Jesus—Pilate in an extraordinary way. Perhaps it was stubbornness, perhaps it was simply retaliation for the implied threat that the leaders would denounce him as 'not a friend of Caesar', but it was still extraordinary. Pilate's words were displayed along a major route into Jerusalem, John the Baptiser's words—whether spoken in the Jezreel Valley or the Jordan Valley—were also on a main thoroughfare.

Pilate's wife had a tormenting dream involving Jesus and she warned her husband not to have anything to do with Him. Pilate would have taken this seriously. The Romans considered dreams to be a form of divine communication, often revealing details of the future. A wife's dream had been considered portentous ever since the assassination of Julius Caesar, some seventy years previously. Calpurnia, Caesar's wife, had a terrible dream about Caesar dying in her arms just the night before he died. Convinced he was about to be killed, she pleaded with him to stay home and not attend the Senate.

Pilate was in a double bind: desperate to release Jesus, convinced of His innocence, he wasn't secure enough in his position to risk the threat of a report to the emperor.

Contrast his insecurity with John the Baptiser's serene sense of security. It didn't trouble John in the least that Jesus was doing as he did. In fact, it probably wouldn't have troubled him if anyone else had started doing what he did—a call for true and heartfelt repentance doesn't leave room for jealousy. Otherwise, it's simply hypocrisy—we haven't washed ourselves in the water and Spirit we're calling others to enjoy. It may seem strange to suggest that repentance is enjoyable—yet the fruits of it are. Moreover, the closer we get to the heart of God, the more we desire for others to experience the same intimacy.

Pilate finally stands against the chief priests but his action comes across as petulant, rather than resounding with integrity: *'What I have written, I have written.'*

Besides these two unmistakeable references to the word *write*, there are actually another four here in these verses as well, all based on Greek 'graphó'. These six usages echo the triplet of references to *the Word* at the very beginning of John's gospel and foreshadow the triplet of references written right at the end:

> *This is the disciple who is bearing witness about these things, and who has **written** these things, and we know that his testimony is true. Now there are also many other things that Jesus did. Were every one of them to be **written**, I suppose that the world itself could not contain the books that would be **written**.*
>
> John 21:24–25[ESV]

Pontius Pilate, despite his annoyance and irritation, proclaimed the Truth he indicated he was so doubtful existed—that Jesus is the king of the Jews.¹²⁴ John the apostle, however, extends the kingship of Jesus much further: in his first and last words, he maintains it covers the entire cosmos.

---

124 It is sometimes maintained that the inscription Pilate wrote is an acronym for YHWH, the usual Hebrew name used when referring to God. This, it is alleged, was the main objection of the chief priests to Pilate's description of the nature of Jesus' crime. This suggestion is, however, difficult to justify. John's gospel gives the closest possibility with YHH, but those letters would refer to *Jesus, the* and *the*. Admittedly *theKing* and *theJews* are both one word in Hebrew, but so is every other word prefixed by 'the'.

7.2 The Place of the Skull

John replied, 'A man can receive only what is given him from heaven. You yourselves can testify that I said, "I am not the Christ, but am sent ahead of Him." The bride belongs to the bridegroom. The friend of the bridegroom stands and listens for him, and is overjoyed to hear the bridegroom's voice. That joy is mine, and it is now complete. He must increase; I must decrease.'

John 3:27-30[BSB]

Then Pilate handed Jesus over to be crucified, and the soldiers took Him away. Carrying His own cross, He went out to The Place of the Skull, which in Hebrew is called 'Golgotha.'

There they crucified Him, and with Him two others, one on each side, with Jesus in the middle.

John 19:16-18[BSB]

HERE IS A STRANGE PARALLEL. The joy of hearing the Bridegroom's voice is matched with the death of Jesus at Golgotha. How can there be any commonality in this pairing?

Now 'Golgotha' is a curious word with paradoxical overtones. It means *place of the skull* and derives from 'gulgoleth', *skull, head* or *census count*. The root of 'gulgoleth' is 'galal', *roll away*. It's related to *dancing*—traditionally involving circular movement—and to *joy*, perhaps through its association with a dance of happiness.

However, 'gulgoleth' also has negative connotations since 'galal' can mean *dung balls* as well as *heap* and *refuse*. Still, back with its positive overtones, 'galal' is *circuit* and also the *territory* enclosing the circuit. In addition, it extends to the *nobility of a person who ruled that territory*.[125]

Further on the positive side, 'galal' comes from 'gol', a word for *rotation*. This root is used various contexts such as *rolling* stones, *spinning* wheels or *twirling* sheaves of wheat to cast off seeds of grain.[126] It's even used for *commit*. David wrote:

> *Commit your way to the Lord; trust in Him, and He will act.*
>
> Psalm 37:5[ESV]

Here 'gol' is the word translated *commit*. Its sense is that of something being *whirled away*, as in the casting off of all the seeds in an evil harvest.[127] We may have sown repeated transgression in life and be due to reap a dark and malevolent harvest, but by repenting and binding ourselves in loyalty to the Lord, the consequences can be mitigated. At Golgotha, the evil harvest we have sown was spun onto Jesus and, through His atonement, the reaping due to appear in our lives was cancelled.

But there's still more.

In its whirling sense, 'gol' can also be the reminder of a stone being propelled from a slingshot, and thus of the famous incident where David confronts Goliath. In fact, some commentators

---

125 See: abarim-publications.com/Meaning/Golgotha.html (accessed 27 November 2023)

126 See: chaimbentorah.com/2024/05/hebrew-word-study-twirling-wheat-gol/ (accessed 20 May 2024)

127 This is a different word from 'paqad', *commit*, in Psalm 31:5 which Jesus quotes just before His death. John does not mention this quote but merely says that Jesus gave up His spirit.

believe 'gulgoleth' actually refers to the place where Goliath's head was buried after David used it as a trophy to intimidate the Jebusites of Jerusalem:

> *David ran and stood over him. He took hold of the Philistine's sword and drew it from the sheath. After he killed him, he cut off his head with the sword…*
>
> *David took the Philistine's head and brought it to Jerusalem; he put the Philistine's weapons in his own tent.*
>
> 1 Samuel 17:51; 54^{NIV}

This is quite a mysterious comment. Twenty years or so before David took the Jebusite city, he apparently already had his eye on it. He took the head from the Valley of Elah to Jerusalem, a distance of some 25 kilometres.[128] Why Jerusalem? At that point in time, it was a hilltop controlled by the Jebusites, situated in the territory of Benjamin on the edge of the desert. Its water supply was problematic—as indicated by the name of its fortress, Zion, *dry* or *parched*. For centuries it was a pagan outpost—under Egyptian control prior to the coming of the Israelites and, once Joshua had defeated its king and armies, reverting to Amorite rulership. Joshua hadn't bothered to take control of it, even when he'd just defeated five Amorite armies and there was no one to oppose him. Nor did any of the judges after Joshua see it as worth the effort. Saul ignored it, even though it was part of his own tribe's allotment. It was clearly not deemed a sufficient prize by anyone. Not, that is, until David decided to lay a claim to it by emplacing Goliath's head outside the gates—as if he's threatening, 'You're next.'

By conquering the city, he could name it after himself. Perhaps that was his long-term motivation and deep-held desire. His ambition

---

128 See: bibleplaces.com/blog/2009/12/where-did-goliaths-head-go/ (accessed 25 May 2024)

was to have a city named after himself. However he could hardly war against any of the tribes of Israel to achieve this. It clearly wouldn't do to rename his original capital Hebron, conquered by Joshua's faithful friend Caleb, as the 'City of David'. But a Jebusite fortress—that was ideal.[129]

Now bear in mind that the Philistines, when they finally killed Saul, put his head in the temple of Dagon[130] and hung his armour in the temple of the Ashtoreths.[131] That was an obvious way of advertising a triumph: when people came to worship, they'd see the spoils on show. It would certainly have been possible for David to do something similar and take Goliath's head to Gibeon, where the Tabernacle was then located. But it is doubtful the priests would have permitted such a display there since it would have defiled the sanctuary.

So David put the trophy of his first victory right next to the place where, years later, he'd propose to build the Temple. Right outside the gates of the city he'd call after himself. This hardly seems

---

[129] Now, lest you think this is too harsh an assessment of David's character and attributes unwarranted and unworthy ambition to him, note his later actions. When Joab was about to take the Ammonite city of Rabbah (the present-day capital of Jordan, Amman), he sent a message to David who had been dallying with Bathsheba in Jerusalem. It was during the siege of Rabbah that Bathsheba's husband, Uriah, was killed by David's order and that Uriah's squadron was sacrificed as collateral damage. The gist of Joab's message is this: 'I've taken the lower city and I'm about to take the citadel. If you don't come right now, I'll be the one credited with its capture and it'll be named after me.' That motivates David to get up and moving. Rather than let Joab take his due, David heads off post haste to Rabbah with the Ark of the Covenant to take command of the army—all just in time to be crowned as its conqueror. His shame over Uriah's death is obvious in the way he projects the blame onto the Ammonites and tortures the population. Modern translations tend to sanitise his actions but the ancient Greek Septuagint made his cruelty quite clear.

[130] 1 Chronicles 10:10

[131] 1 Samuel 31:10. As pointed out in *The Summoning of Time: John 2 and 20*, the Ashtoreths of Beit She'an included the war goddess Anat.

coincidental since it would achieve effectively the same result as the Philistine way of dedicating conquests to their patron deities.

Whether the design for the Temple was conceived in David's mind or as a result of the Holy Spirit's inspiration is an open question, since 1 Chronicles 28:12 does not specify clearly.[132] God, after all, makes it perfectly clear He has never asked anyone to build a Temple for Him and, in fact, He forbids David as a *'man of blood'* from doing so. He permits Solomon to do so, but this is obviously not ideal. Just as God permitted the kingship to be instituted, despite warning against it, so He allowed the Temple to be constructed.

Throughout the history of Israel, the Tabernacle had been a tent, a symbol of God dwelling amongst His people. Until the time the Ark of the Covenant was taken into battle and lost to the Philistines, the Tabernacle and the Ark had been together. Once the Ark was returned, it was kept at Kiriath-Jearim[133] while the Tabernacle had moved from Shiloh to Gibeon. David sets about reuniting the Ark and the Tabernacle—in his new capital, Jerusalem.

When the removal of the Ark from Kiriath-Jearim to Jerusalem has fatal consequences, the motivation of David's heart is revealed.

> *And David was afraid of the Lord that day, and he said, 'How can the ark of the Lord come to me?'*
>
> 2 Samuel 6:9[ESV]

Those last two words, *'to me'*, suggest that the motivation behind David's desire to bring the Ark to Jerusalem was at least

---

[132] Despite the capitalisation of 'Spirit' in the New International Version, the Hebrew is not altogether clear. There is no unequivocal statement that the *Holy* Spirit dropped the idea into David's mind. It could have been a desire of his own spirit in operation.

[133] Also called Baalah of Judah.

as much about his own glory as it was about the Lord's. David grew increasingly afraid of God as he aged. After his affair with Bathsheba and his murder of Uriah, he decided to conduct a census of the fighting men. Joab—surely the least spiritually sensitive of men in all Israel at the time—nevertheless has enough wits about him to protest that this will be an affront to God. David overrules him as well as the commanders with him and demands that the census go ahead. Nearly ten months later, once the numbers are in, David realises he's sinned and is horrified at the three options God presents to him by way of atonement: three years of famine, three months of pursuit by enemies, or three days of plague.

It's that last option that takes place. The Angel of Death comes to Jerusalem with his sword poised over the city—and stops, at the Lord's command. David and his officials see the angel there, awaiting further direction. The angel had paused over the threshing floor of the Jebusite king, Araunah.[134]

David approached Araunah who was threshing wheat with his sons.[135] At the direction of the prophet Gad, David bought the field for 600 gold shekels and built an altar there and the plague was stopped. It would appear from this that David paid an atonement fee for about 16,000 men through this action.[136] Had he paid an atonement fee before insisting on the census count, none of the three unpleasant options would have descended on him. It was not forbidden to take a census, but an atonement had to be paid.

That threshing floor David bought eventually became the site of the Temple and, just beyond it, was Golgotha, *the place of the*

---

134 Also called Ornan.
135 1 Chronicles 12:20
136 A gold shekel was originally the same value as a silver shekel but came, over time, to be 40:3 of a silver shekel. Perhaps 16,000 fighting men constituted the inhabitants of Jerusalem.

skull. Even if Goliath's head had not been buried there, there were issues with David's choice. A threshing floor belonging to royalty would have been a place of worship, judgment and divination involving pagan gods.

Now let me recap from earlier: 'gulgoleth' means not only *skull* or *head* but also *census count*. It derives from 'gol' which refers to *whirling* things like *stones from a slingshot* or *grain being cast off as it is threshed*. It refers to *rolling away*, with a distinct resonance of *removing the reproach of sin*. All of these elements come into play at Golgotha—including, most importantly, the implied call for *atonement*.

At Golgotha, Jesus makes atonement for the sin of the world. He rolls away the reproach of David's sin and the defilement David brought on the nation through his actions with the head of Goliath and his unwise census-taking. It would appear, in retrospect, that David's long-term strategy was to have Goliath's head buried right outside the Temple gates as a reminder, to his own generation and also those yet-unborn, of his victory over the six-fingered giant. Such a memorial is ultimately not about God's glory but David's.[137]

'He must increase,' John the Baptiser had said. 'I must decrease.' Ministry is about the glory of God, not about the glory of self. When the taint of self-aggrandisement comes in, it's a short road to corruption.

Now, of course, Jesus through the power of His atonement did far, far more than just dealing with David's desecration. That was merely part of His healing of history and a tiny fraction of

---

[137] We begin to see that Absalom, in creating a memorial to himself, didn't just conceive of it out of thin air. He had an excellent role model in his father and in Saul before him.

the story of redeeming us all. But John's mention of Golgotha harks back to the mixture of leavened and unleavened motives in David's heart, to the pure and the corrupt, to the holy and unholy, and to the godly and ungodly.

And thus, it speaks to us whose hearts are no less sullied than David's. Even if he did start out with the stunning commendation of being a *'man after God's own heart'*.

7.3 Adversaries

There are echoes of David's transgressions all the way through the scenes involving Pilate, some of which we will examine shortly. However, there are other themes entwined in with these allusions to the *head*. In the wider context of *birth* and *piercing*—two of the dominant motifs within these chiastic chapters—there appears to be another indirect pointer to Anat, the warmonger goddess hidden in the shadows of John's second chapter.

In terms of skulls and birth and spears, there's an apparent sidelong reference to Athena, goddess of wisdom. According to legend, her birth came about when she sprang, full grown, from the skull of Zeus, holding a spear and armoured for battle. Athena is the Greek equivalent of the Canaanite warrior goddess Anat and also the Egyptian deity of shroud-wrappings, Neith.

In this allusion, there is a subtle rebuke reminiscent of Paul's far more forthright declaration:

> *Jews demand signs and Greeks look for wisdom, but we preach Christ crucified: a stumbling block to Jews and foolishness to Gentiles, but to those whom God has called, both Jews and Greeks, Christ the power of God and the wisdom of God. For the foolishness of God is wiser than*

> human wisdom, and the weakness of God is stronger than human strength.
>
> 1 Corinthians 1:22–25^{NIV}

Jesus was buried in the vicinity of Golgotha. More than just a reference to Goliath, it's a name that holds the same implicit promise God gave the people at Gilgal. There they renewed the covenant with Him on first entering their inheritance of the Promised Land, and He announced:

> 'Today I have rolled away the reproach of Egypt from you.'
>
> Joshua 5:9^{ESV}

Ultimately the Hebrew word for 'Egypt' derives in a long chain from a word for *adversary*, so this word spoken to Joshua is prophetic of the power of the Cross at Golgotha to remove the accusations of the enemy from our lives. That is a joy for us, when we are born again as we enter by faith into the wound in Jesus' side. But, strange as it seems, it also held out a prospect of joy for Jesus:

> *Because of the joy awaiting Him, He endured the cross, disregarding its shame.*
>
> Hebrews 12:2^{NLT}

And indeed it was the joy of the Bridegroom that Jesus was looking forward to. John the Baptiser was joyful simply in being the Friend of the Bridegroom. How much more joyful would the Bridegroom Himself have been as He contemplated the birth of His perfect, spotless, radiant Bride?

John the Baptiser declares his joy is complete and states: *'He must increase, I must decrease.'* Jeremy Chance Springfield mentions that this is a pointer to baptism: 'To be filled with the Spirit requires the unbecoming of self, the emptying, the washing away, so that we can become our true regenerate self, full to overflowing with the cleansing, revitalising power of Jesus, the Living Water. His very words echo the spiritual event that happens in the act of baptism: the individual is diminishing while the Spirit is increasing upon him! This is the very concept of… "unbecoming."[138]

Yet we see in the 'unbecoming' of Jesus—His death of self that testifies to His lifelong death to self—our own salvation. His emptying of self in an atoning sacrifice won for us eternal life and miraculous redemption.

---

138 See: Jeremy Chance Springfield, randomgroovybiblefacts.com/waters_of_unbecoming.html (accessed 10 May 2024)

7.4 Mathematically Rolled Away

The opening verses of John's third chapter[139] are structurally dominated by the number 44. While for us, in the third millennium, it's at best somewhat eccentric to devise a numerical underlay for a literary work, it was not so in the first century. The fusion of words and numbers was not simply common across the ancient world, east and west, it was expected. John's audience wouldn't have taken him seriously if he didn't display various arithmetic building blocks in the architecture of his gospel to confirm his text. Numbers frequently had symbolic meaning that, today, is mostly lost to us—but can be reconstructed, given sufficient context.

Verses 1 and 2 combined are 44 words.

Verses 3 and 4 combined are 44 words.

Verses 7, 8 and 9 combined are also 44 words.

In verses 5, 6 and 7, Jesus says 44 words.

Verse 5 itself is 22 or 23 words,
    for a total in the first five verses of 110 or 111 words.

Verses 17 through to 21 are also 110 words.

Likewise, verses 13 through 18 are 110 words.

---

[139] See Appendix 1 for details of the word and letter counts for each verse.

Verses 10 and 11 combined are 33 words.

Verses 11 and 12 combined are also 33 words.

So too, verses 13 and 14 are 33 words.

Verses 15, 16 and 17 total 55 words.

Verses 11 through 14 total 66 words.

Verses 7 through 11 total 77 words.

Verses 15 through 18 also total 77 words.

Verses 13 through to 17 total 88 words.

Verses 9 to 15 total 99 words.

Verses 14 to 19 total 121 words.

Verses 11 through to 17 also total 121 words.

These are the totals occurring up to the end of the scene with Nicodemus. All this suggests a numerical sub-structure based on multiples of 11. In the next pericope—where John the Baptiser discusses his joy as the friend of the Bridegroom—there are further examples of this patterning. However, in that section, multiples of 17 predominate.

Yet, given the repetition of 44 in the opening lines, our attention is surely directed specifically to that number.

Now I might have been perplexed by this numerical setup, except for the fact multiples of 11—and especially multiples of 22—are so very common in the structure of medieval poetry.[140] Having noted their presence and analysed their nature in that context back when I was teaching mathematics, there was, to my mind, an obvious and immediate avenue to pursue. In medieval poetry, the multiples of 22 are generally indicative of the 'Wheel of Fate',[141] a

---

[140] See: Anne Hamilton, *Gawain and the Four Daughters of God: The Testimony of Mathematics in Cotton Nero A.x*, Armour Books 2014

[141] Also called the Wheel of Fortune.

concept referring to the rising and falling of kings and princes to and from obscurity as far up as the highest rank in the land.

The mathematics of a circle was used during the Middle Ages in lyrical design to show when the wheel begins to turn. The poet would describe either the beginning of the hero's rise or else his fall on a line numbering that corresponded to $7/22$ of the length of the poem. Now $7/22$ is simply the inverse of $22/7$, the well-known approximation for π originally discovered by Archimedes. It symbolises a circle.

While I doubt even the faintest whiff of the 'Wheel of Fate' is present in John's gospel, I nonetheless think that these opening multiples of 44 are meant to direct our attention towards circles. Now it is possible a *wheel*, 'galgal', which also means *whirling dust, whirlwind, chaff, stubble*—fits the hidden motif of the *threshing floor*. The gematria[142] of 'galgal' is 66 and, while that number does appear as a combined total in these consecutive sequences, it does so only once.[143] So, it's close in my view, but not quite close enough.[144]

Now in fact, there is a Hebrew word deliberately evoked here with a gematria of 44 that means *move in a circle*. It is 'chul'[145] which also means to *go around a circuit, whirl, dance, writhe in*

---

142   Gematria is the ancient practice of assigning specific numbers to letters and thereby calculating the values of words. It can easily slide into occult interpretations; but just because it has been counterfeited doesn't mean it is completely ungodly. Its limited use throughout Scripture is clear, and is often understood to be part of one of the four layers of meaning: 'peshat', *surface*; 'remez', *hint* or *deep*; 'derash', *comparative, or similar circumstances or context*; 'sod', *secret*.

143   'Gol' by itself, the word for *whirling* stones from slingshots or grain from sheaves, has a gematria of 33.

144   Another similar Hebrew word with a numerical value of 66 is 'lil', *turn* or *wind*. The word for *night* is thought to come from 'lil' and to express the idea of a *turning away of the light*.

145   Also spelled 'chil'.

childbirth, to tremble, to be firm and mighty, to wait, to surround, to enclose.

Many of those meanings show that 'chul' is essentially synonymous with 'gol', along with the additional overtone of *bearing a child*. This is just a perfect mathematical underlay for the opening sequence of a story about being *born again*.

Now *fortress*, 'chel', derives from 'chul' and so does 'chayil', which describes the *competence* and *capability* of armies, the *valiant* heart of a warrior or the *valour* of a champion, the *excellence* of a force or, on rare occasions, the *virtue* of a woman.[146]

The word 'chayil' is the perfect description of Jesus: He is a tower of strength even while writhing in pain as He brings to new birth all those who believe in Him.

To complete the mathematical imagery of a circle, it should be possible to find multiples of 7 in this chapter as well as multiples of 22. There are in fact 92 multiples in total throughout this portion of the text to be found in various combinations of consecutive verses; they consist of 52 different factors other than 7. These totals are the following numbers multiplied by 7:—4, 5, 6, 9, 10, 11, 13, 14, 15, 17, 18, 20, 21, 24, 25, 27, 28, 29, 30, 31, 32, 33, 34, 35, 36, 37, 54, 55, 59, 60, 61, 62, 65, 67, 68, 69, 70, 71, 72, 73, 75, 76, 77, 80, 84, 85, 86, 92, 94, 95, 98, 105.

Of these, the most common, appearing 5 times, is 20x7, closely followed by 77x7 which appears 4 times. 77x7 may be intended to evoke the mathematical motif for 'forgiveness', referring to the famous reply of Jesus when Simon Peter asked Him how

---

146 There are over 220 usages of 'chayil' but just twice, in Proverbs 31:10 and 31:29, is it translated *virtue* or *noble*. Because, after all, there couldn't possibly be a woman of valour, could there? Sarcasm aside, the translators of Scripture are often the real problem when it comes to the expression of patriarchy in the Bible, not the text itself.

many times he should forgive a brother who apologises.[147] Now because of the ambiguity regarding mathematical operations in the ancient world, Jesus could have answered, 'Seventy times seven' or alternatively, 'Seventy plus seven'. This accounts for the differing translations of 490 or 77.

77x7 has substantially different overtones, however, and if it is intended to remind us of 777, then it refers to the Armour of God. 777 is a structural number embedded in the first verse of Genesis,[148] as well as the first verse of John's gospel and also the passage in Paul's letter to the Ephesians about the Armour of God.[149] It refers to covenantal defence. And there can be no greater protection than to be hidden in Christ, abiding by faith in the wound in His side, as once Moses was tucked in the cleft in the rock as the glory of the Lord was revealed to him. It would thus be a lovely mathematical touch here in chiastic match for John's description of the spearwound that births the Bride.

---

147 Matthew 18:22

148 This is not surprising since the gematria of the Hebrew phrase 'in the firmament of heaven' is 777.

149 See: *The Elijah Tapestry: John 1 and 21*, the first volume in this series.

7.5 The King's Crown

The soldiers twisted together a crown of thorns and placed it on His head, and put a purple cloak on Him.

John 19:2[NASB]

Although the soldiers mocked Jesus with the apparel of royalty, it was on the hill of Golgotha that He was officially announced as the 'King of the Jews'. Pilate did so in his proclamation of 'the crime' of Jesus. It was a task that should have been fulfilled by Caiaphas—the high priest whose name is the same as Cephas, the Aramaic equivalent of Peter. Cephas was the name given by Jesus to Simon the fisherman when he declared that Jesus was the Messiah. The word 'cephas' is not merely a *rock* but a *cornerstone*, the very first block laid down in the foundation of a building—a building made of living stones, the church.

In granting Simon the same name as the high priest, Jesus indicated that Caiaphas had missed his calling: his destiny was to announce the coming of the Messiah to the Jewish people, but he forfeited it through his desire to retain power. Pilate therefore became the agent of a public announcement, writing the sign that was affixed to the Cross on Golgotha.

It was here, as we've seen, that it was likely Goliath's head was taken by David after the battle in the Valley of Elah. Goliath was a

Philistine, one of the sea people who lived in a league of cities on the Mediterranean coast. They came from the Aegean, suggesting that Goliath's ancestry was, at least in part, Greek. Scripture also implies that he was descended from the Anakim, the giants Caleb expelled from Hebron—a city named for their forefather, Arba.

When Caleb conquered Hebron, the displaced giants went to three of the cities of the Philistines—Ashdod, Gaza and Goliath's hometown Gath.[150] Goliath therefore appears to have a mixed bloodline of Philistine and Anakim. The Philistine giants were also considered to descend from the Rephaim,[151] a warrior clan that included the monstrous King Og.

The Hebrew word 'anak' means *long-necked* or *necklace*[152] and derives from a word for *strangle*. However, Anak is clearly not Hebrew in origin. It's a foreign name and is thought to derive from Greek 'anax', *god, hero* or *master of the house*.[153] Anakim would therefore simply mean *kings, rulers* or *lords* and be a title similar to Pharaoh,[154] Abimelech[155] or Araunah.[156]

Goliath, a descendent of Greek-Philistine heritage from the giant Anak, *king*, was killed by David and his head taken to Jerusalem.

Jesus, a descendent of David, was declared *king* in three languages including Greek by Pilate[157] at the place where Goliath's head was believed to have been buried.

---

150 Joshua 11:22
151 2 Samuel 21:15–22
152 The root of *neck* in English may be 'anak'.
153 See: allpropastors.org/the-nephilim-and-the-sons-of-god/ (accessed 25 May 2024)
154 Hereditary title of the rulers of Egypt meaning *great house*.
155 Hereditary title of the rulers of Gerar meaning *my father is king*.
156 Hereditary title of the Jebusite rulers of Jerusalem, meaning either *Yahweh is firm* (somewhat surprising!) or *tall ash tree*.
157 Pilate probably conducted his entire interrogation with Jesus in Greek.

The Greek word, 'anax', is essentially cognate with the Hebrew word, 'baal'. It was on Golgotha and later in the garden outside the tomb that Jesus so comprehensively defeated Baal-Hadad, the king of the Canaanite gods and, by extension, the chief of the principalities of the nations.[158] However it is not just these territorial angel-shepherds and spirit-kings that Jesus triumphed over, He also showed His lordship over the demonic hybrids that were their descendants—the Anakim, the demi-gods and heroes who claimed to be kings of the earth. The significance of Golgotha is not simply that it reinforces David's victory over Goliath, but that it speaks to two sets of kings of the earth:

- first, the angelic powers who were assigned rulership of the Gentiles but who abandoned their roles as guardians and began to desire worship in their own right

- second, the demonic powers who were the product of an angelic-human mating[159]

David got it right, prophetically speaking: it was at Golgotha that the King of the Universe would triumph over the angelic principalities and demonic powers who ruled the world. It was there Jesus crushed the head of the serpent who had conspired to thwart God's plans for humanity in Eden and who has tempted each man and woman down the ages.

But David also got it terribly wrong. It wasn't by taking life that the redemption of God's people would be won, but by giving it as a ransom for many. It wasn't with a sword that the King would extend His rule, but with a Cross of love.

---

158 See *The Summoning of Time: John 2 and 20*, the previous book in this series.

159 Note the distinction. Principalities are spiritual powers who rule over the nations. They are fallen angels. Demons on the other hand are the spirits of the dead offspring of angels and humans. They are hybrid entities that seek re-embodiment in matter, preferably walking, talking flesh.

7.6 The Bridegroom's Crown

THE CROWN OF THORNS IS USUALLY SEEN in the light of Jesus as king. However it's also indicative of the crown and garments of a bridegroom. It was normal in that era, when the wedding day arrived, that the bridegroom would dress in colourful, festive apparel and wear a crown. The wealthy had a circlet of gold or silver, while the poor chose a wreath of flowers twisted together or a headband of braided wool.

The meaning of Golgotha, *place of the skull*, and its derivation from things that *roll, circle,* or *perform a circuit* points us further towards this piercing crown Jesus wore. Yet there's more symbolism here than the coronet of a king or a bridegroom; there's also the headwear of a priest:

> *I delight greatly in the Lord;*
> *my soul rejoices in my God.*
> *For He has clothed me with garments of salvation*
> *and arrayed me in a robe of His righteousness,*
> *as a bridegroom adorns his head like a priest,*
> *and as a bride adorns herself with her jewels.*
>
> Isaiah 61:10[NIV]

Golgotha was also not far from the garden of Gethsemane, *oil press*. Gethsemane's first syllable, 'geth-', comes from 'gath', *winepress*. Once more we are reminded of Goliath—through his hometown of Gath. But we're also reminded yet again of Anat who waded thigh-deep in the blood of her guests, just as farmers stomped grape juice past their knees in their winepresses.[160]

Perhaps the pressing down of grapes to increase the volume of wine is a subtle reflection of the words of John the Baptiser:

He must increase; I must decrease.

John 3:30[BSB]

Wine, after all, like myrrh was a symbol of joy for the Jews. Both wine and myrrh occur in this same scene when a sour wine mixture is offered to Jesus on a stalk of hyssop.

---

160 See: *The Summoning of Time: John 2 and 20*, the previous book in this series.

7.7 The Bride's Mikvah

BAPTISM IS A SYMBOL OF PURIFICATION. Just as the waters of the flood cleansed the world back in the days of Noah, so baptism is a cleansing, a sign of repentance and an indication that sin has been removed.

> *Those flood waters were like baptism that now saves you. But baptism is more than just washing your body. It means turning to God with a clear conscience, because Jesus Christ was raised from death.*
>
> 1 Peter 3:21[CEV]

The rite of purification for a Jewish bride is like baptism. Before the wedding the bride immerses herself in a mikvah. This is a pool especially built to hold purifying water. The stone jars at Cana used for ceremonial washing were probably containers to fill a mikvah.[161] In addition, stone was considered appropriate for the storage of 'living water' while pottery vessels were not.[162]

The immersion in the mikvah prior to a marriage is not only a preparation for the wedding day itself but is also seen as the bride's own personal Yom Kippur, her own individual day of atonement,

---

[161] The average bathtub holds about 200 litres of water—similar to the capacity of one of the stone jars at Cana.

a day when she will be 'reborn' as a unit together with her new husband and can approach life with a fresh slate.[163]

Here, once again, we have the very images John has tied together throughout his chiastic parallels in the first three and last three chapters. His opening with John the Baptiser occurs on Yom Kippur in a scene where the waters of baptism are prominent; he moves on to tell us of water for purification at Cana, even while a wedding is taking place. He then links water and Spirit to being born again. As this picture is building, he confirms it at the end of his gospel with bridal references from the Song of Songs, a pierced side gushing with blood-spirit and water, a description of a king, priest and bridegroom, and a mention of oil of joy in such quantity it can only be for the celebration of the Marriage of the Lamb.

John the Baptiser mentions the Bridegroom three times in one verse, in reply to a question about baptism:

> *The bride belongs to the bridegroom. The friend of the bridegroom stands and listens for him, and is overjoyed to hear the bridegroom's voice.*
>
> John 3:29[BSB]

---

[162] According to drivethruhistoryadventures.com/stone-jars-ritual-washing-water-wine-miracle-cana/ (accessed 30 November 2023), stone vessels were common in Judea for ritual purposes. The Law of Moses indicated stone would not become impure, unlike often-used pottery (Leviticus 6:28, 11:33–36). Additionally, running water or living water was considered pure, and collection of water in a stone cistern could be used for purification purposes (Leviticus 11:36, 15:13). This 'living water' could be stored in a large stone water jar, which would function like a cistern holding ritually clean water, then later it could be used for purification. While the use of stone vessels is not apparent from the Hebrew Bible and must be implied, sources in the Mishnah make it clear that this was the understanding during the Roman period.

[163] See: chabad.org/theJewishWoman/article_cdo/aid/5368691/jewish/Mikvah-Before-a-Wedding.htm (accessed 15 April 2024)

Yet perhaps there is an additional emblem of bridal union in this chapter beyond the simple immersion in water that is part of the preparation for a marriage. A Jewish wedding ceremony of today is not complete without exuberant dancing that involves the bridal couple being lifted up on chairs,[164] symbolising the mutual uplift that the newlyweds should extend to each other throughout their marriage. Although the Talmud does not refer to this lifting as an ancient practice, it does comment that it's unwise to lift the bride and groom and carry them around on a rabbi's shoulders—surely an unnecessary remark unless it was being done at least occasionally.[165] Moreover, the bride is described as being seated on a throne as a queen and sometimes the groom is with her as they are feted like a royal couple.

If this dance that involves lifting up either on chairs or shoulders goes back to the first century, then John has even more profoundly linked the *lifting up* of the crucifixion, resurrection and ascension to a wedding.[166] When he describes the Son of Man being lifted up, he uses the Greek word 'hypsoō', meaning both *lift* and *exalt*. Of the several choices he could have made for *lift*, this is the only one that shares the same double meaning as its Hebrew cognate, 'nāsā', *lift* or *exalt*.

Not coincidentally, one of the Hebrew words for *married* is 'nasu', derived from 'nāsā'.

---

164 See: smashingtheglass.com/dancing-hora-jewish-wedding-traditions-explained-9/ (accessed 15 April 2024)

165 See:chabad.org/library/article_cdo/aid/4613565/jewish/Why-Lift-the-Bride-and-Groom-on-Chairs-at-Jewish-Weddings.htm (accessed 15 April 2024)

166 For 'lift up' in John 3:14 as meaning the continuous event of crucifixion, resurrection and ascension, see: Raymond E. Brown, *The Gospel According to John*, vol. 29a in *The Anchor Bible*, eds. William Albright and David Freeman (New York, NY: Doubleday, 1966)

7.8 The 'Invincible Sun'

> *He was put to death in a mortal body but was brought to life by the Spirit, in which He went and made a proclamation to those imprisoned spirits who disobeyed long ago in the days of Noah, when God waited patiently while the ark was being built. In it a few, that is, eight persons, were saved by water. Baptism, which is symbolised by that water, now saves you also, not by removing dirt from the body, but by asking God for a clear conscience based on the resurrection of Jesus, the Messiah, who has gone to heaven and is at the right hand of God, where angels, authorities, and powers have been made subject to Him.*
>
> 1 Peter 3:18–22^{ISV}

THE IMPRISONED SPIRITS REFERENCED IN this passage have long been understood to be the same fallen angels that Peter mentions in his second letter as being sent down to Tartarus.[167] This means that, strictly speaking, they are not demons but rather the fathers of demons. They are the angelic powers who descended to earth to consort with human women. Demons are their offspring—or more accurately, demons are the *spirits* of the children of this angelic-human mating. The physical flesh of these hybrids

---

[167] 2 Peter 2:4

was destroyed in the flood, but their spirits remain, seeking re-embodiment. Tartarus is a Greek word for the lowest level of hell, the prison where the elder-gods, the titans, were incarcerated. Thus Peter implicitly equated these fallen angels with the titans.

When we become convinced such beings are merely legend, we miss the great cosmic war that Jesus was engaged in. It didn't start at the Cross; nor did it end with His resurrection. Each of His miraculous signs was a battle in its own right. Each of His 'I Am' statements was a take-down of a different adversary in this spiritual conflict. Here in this section John lays the groundwork for a revelation to be unveiled later in his gospel: 'I Am the Light of the World.'[168]

In the previous chiastic sections, he brought together elements of *light* and *verdict*, along with a prominent mention of Roman soldiers. Now he's emphasising *bride* and *covenant*—with the bridal allusions increasing throughout the crucifixion scene until they culminate in that triumphant word of consummation, 'Kalot!', *It is finished, My bride.*[169]

In the culture of the day, this particular combination of symbols would have been unmistakeable: just as 'born again' would have reminded John's readers of twice-born Dionysius, so this cluster of motifs would have reminded them of the Persian sun-god Mithra, known among the Romans as Mehr or Mithras. The legionnaires, more than any other group of Roman society, were devoted to this deity who claimed the title, *The Light of the World*. And Jewish men, chafing under the rule of occupation that required

---

168 John 8:12[ESV]
169 The translation of Brian Simmons in *The Book of John: Eternal Love*, Broadstreet Publishing Group 2016, includes 'My bride,' along with 'It is finished!' because the Aramaic 'kalot' has this dual meaning.

them to carry a soldier's pack for a mile on request, would have known about the beliefs of their task-masters. They'd have known the outline of the Mithraic religion, if not the details. They'd have known Mithraic temples had a bath area, not unlike a mikvah.[170] Such waters mimicked baptism in that they were deemed a ritual cleansing in preparation for a new level of initiation into the Mithraic mysteries.

John wants his readers to know that Mithras is an imposter, a counterfeit of the True Light, a fraudulent claimant to a title that rightfully belongs to God alone. Even at this point in his narrative, even without mentioning the explicit title, there are sufficient clues for his original audience of readers to make the right connections.

Devotees of Mithras, the so-called Invincible Sun, underwent seven degrees[171] of initiation:

- Raven
- Bride
- Soldier
- Lion
- Persian
- Sun-Runner
- Father.

---

170 William Barclay, *Turning to God: A study in conversion in the book of Acts and today*, St Andrew Press, 1978
171 Very little is known about the ceremonies involved. If we did know more, perhaps we would see further references in John's record of the crucifixion to Jesus' triumph over Mithras.

Taking a wider view into John's last three chapters we see how Jesus counters these stages.[172] He is like the 'eater of death', the carrion-feeding raven, who swallows up Death in victory; He is explicitly and implicitly, repeatedly, identified as the Bridegroom who is coming for His bride; He is the soldier, the warrior, who has laid down His life to terminate the enemy.

The Roman troops would have considered what Jesus was doing at the Cross as 'devotio'—in their culture, this was an extreme offering to the gods by a battle commander who vowed to sacrifice his own life along with the enemy in exchange for a victory.

Jesus was also the Lion of Judah. Moreover He was prophesied by Malachi to be the Sun of Righteousness with healing in His wings—not as a fluttering bird, but by dispensing healing through the 'feathers' on the 'wings' of His prayer shawl. This is why so many people wanted to touch the hem of His garment—they wanted to unite their pleas for healing with His prayers through grasping at the knotted fringe that He would have fingered as He prayed.

There might also be a pun on a pun when it comes to the degree called 'Persians'. In the last days of Babylon, on the night before its overthrow by Cyrus, strange unearthly writing appeared on the wall of the banqueting hall where King Belshazzar was carousing with his guests. MENE, MENE, TEKEL, PARSIN said the writing.

---

172   Of course, Jesus is the Lion of the Tribe of Judah, but if that allusion exists in these pericopes, I haven't seen it. Sun-runner may refer to the rising of the sun while Father, of course, is referred to during the resurrection scene in the garden when Jesus tells her to inform His brothers and sisters He is going to His Father and their Father. In addition, since John clearly expected His readers to be acquainted with the other gospels, they would have been aware of the wonderful words of forgiveness, *'Father, forgive them, for they know not what they do.'*

When the prophet Daniel was called to interpret the writing, he translated the last word as 'peres', *division*, and also as a pun on *Persians*. Thus the *division* of Jesus' clothing among the soldiers might be meant to be a pointer to a similar pun.[173]

I suspect the unnamed 'Prince of Persia' who resisted the angel Gabriel for 21 days and who blocked his access to Daniel was Mithras.[174] Most importantly, Mithras is a deity of covenants, oaths and contracts. To understand the 'new covenant' in the Blood of Jesus, we have to be able to distinguish between covenant and contract. Most Christian believers today behave as if they were fundamentally the same—perhaps with the proviso that a covenant is an especially solemn and more binding contract. In other words, it's just harder to get out of.

In fact, a true covenant is impossible to get out of, short of divine intervention. A true covenant involves indissoluble unity with another—that's why one of the names for the memorial of the Lord's Supper is communion, *with union.*

A true covenant can be breached—with disastrous consequences—but it can't be undone. It covers the descendants of the partners who swear the covenant oaths, including the blessings and curses. Those pledges are binding on subsequent generations. They do not fade with the passage of time.

This isn't an especially serious or sacred contract—this is qualitatively and quantitatively different. More significant still,

---

173 It's drawing a long bow, admittedly, since we're moving from Greek back to the Hebrew quote from the psalms, then to a cognate in Aramaic that has a potential double meaning as specified by Daniel. On the other hand, the fall of the demonic kingdom was likened in the Book of Revelation to the fall of Babylon, so perhaps such subtlety is indeed built into the story of the Cross.

174 I deduce this because one of the Persian words for *prince* is 'mir', sounding very much like Mehr, the other name for Mithra.

there are certain actions that we can undertake in complete ignorance that bring us into covenant with another person or another spirit. Sex actualises covenantal union. Crossing over the threshold of certain temples actualises covenantal union.

When the question of circumcision—a sign of covenant with God—arose in the early church and the Council of Jerusalem debated the issue, a letter was authorised saying that circumcision was not a requirement for Gentile believers to participate in the church. However:

> *It seemed good to the Holy Spirit and to us not to burden you with anything beyond the following requirements: You are to abstain from food sacrificed to idols, from blood, from the meat of strangled animals and from sexual immorality. You will do well to avoid these things.*
>
> Acts 15:28–29^{NIV}

It might seem like a strange list. But it isn't. Those items were a contemporary inventory of unholy covenantal actions. So what the Council was really saying can be summarised as: you don't need to demonstrate a covenant with God through circumcision, but you do need to avoid any actions that would bring you into covenant with any other gods.

That's why I mentioned crossing the threshold of temples. Because that's implied but not spelled out in the Council's list of things to avoid. I've heard more than one tragic story, including a fatal one,[175] about crossing temple thresholds—and, although the people involved did not understand the safeguards outlined by the Council of Jerusalem or know of the prohibitions about reviling ungodly beings in Jude 1:8–10 and 2 Peter 2:10–12, nevertheless

---

175 The fatal incident followed the exact outline of the consequences implied in Jude 1:11.

there are clear indications that the Holy Spirit warned those involved not to proceed.

Like Anat, Mithras was seen as legitimising the rule of the king, as well as a protector of his favourites. He was invoked by warriors before battle and so became known as a god of war. Thus we can see that Jesus in His death and resurrection is not merely in conflict with Baal-Hadad, the so-called 'Cloud-rider', along with his sister-bride Anat, but also with Dionysius the alleged 'twice-born' as well as Mithras. But, of course, as we shall eventually see in later books in this series, these are not the only powers He took on at this time. They had allies near and far—and they would even make common cause with their enemies when it become obvious that Jesus was a threat to their rule over the nations.

7.9 The King of the Jews

The predominant numerical pattern in the Nicodemus story is, as we've seen, based on multiples of 11. This design feature is not limited to the beginning of the third chapter. There are another 27 such multiples at the end, underlying the structure of the episode with John the Baptiser.[176]

The other characteristic of the mathematical architecture is multiples of 17. Given its prominence in the very first verse of John's gospel as well as in the final chapter, this is not unexpected.[177] In fact, there are 23 sets of consecutive verses where the word total is a multiple of 17. There are even two instances of 153: the combined word total of verses 12 to 19, and the combined word total of verses 19 to 26.[178]

These two significant numbers appear together in the gematria of the phrase 'Jesus of Nazareth, King of the Jews.'

---

176 Six of these multiples cross from one pericope, that of the scene with Nicodemus, to the next, the scene with John the Baptiser.

177 See: *The Elijah Tapestry: John 1 and 21*, the first book in this series.

178 There are also two instances of 265, thus evoking the famous ratio $^{265}/_{153}$ which has approximated $\sqrt{3}$ since the time of Archimedes when 153 was known as 'the measure of the fish'.

The numerical value of the phrase *Jesus of Nazareth* is 2197. *The King of the Jews* has a total of 3413.
Altogether the combination yields 5610.

The factors of 2197 are 13x13x13. There are many possible verbal interpretations of 13, but I'm going to choose the Hebrew word 'ahava'—thus making *Jesus of Nazareth* numerically equal to *love x love x love*. Isn't that simply exquisite?

3413 is a prime number, thus it has no factors other than itself and 1.

The factors of 5610 are 2x3x5x11x17 and this can be reformatted as 15 x 17 x 22, highlighting both 22 and 17, the mathematical design elements of the third chapter.

Now 15 is the value of 'Yah', the short form of Yahweh, the name frequently used for God. The number 17, on the other hand, is—as pointed out in *The Elijah Tapestry*—the value of the archaic form of the true sacred name of God, Ehyeh.[179] Yahweh is NOT the name God used to identify Himself to Moses at the burning bush. It's a simple grammatical step removed from I AM. Yahweh means *He is*, not *I am*. God instructed Moses to use 'Yahweh' to refer to Him when he was speaking to the Israelites, but it is NOT the name He called Himself when He introduced Himself to Moses. That was: 'Ehyeh asher Ehyeh', I AM WHO I AM, I WILL BE WHO I WILL BE.

So, it's highly doubtful the name 'Yahweh' is encoded as the acronym YHWH in this trilingual inscription by Pilate, as some commentators suggest. Nevertheless, it does have two numerical factors, 15 and 17, built into it that both point to the Father.

---

179 This archaic form is 'aahweh'. See, for example: theopolisinstitute.com/leithart_post/17-and-26/ (accessed 23 August 2024) 'Ehyeh' is derived from and sometimes rendered 'Hayah'.

Perhaps to confirm that 17 does indeed point to Ehyeh, there are three sets of word totals that add up to 59. These are verses 20 through 22, and 21 through 23 as well as 22 to 25. One appearance means very little, twice may be coincidence but three times? No, that's deliberate. However 59 is so mysterious in symbolism, I can find no word fitting John's theme with an appropriate gematria. Nor can I uncover a meaning within the realm of mathematics that might suggest its purpose. I therefore tentatively suggest it is a reference to the 59th word in Genesis: 'ehyeh'.

I also suggest that both 15 and 22 may allude to the Feast of the Passover. The date of the Passover which was always on 15 Nisan. And the Hebrew word for *festival* or *feast*, 'chag', while its gematria is *not* 22, nevertheless derives from a root meaning *to dance in a circle*.

Now looking at the end of the gospel rather than the beginning, the chiastic match for the third chapter runs backward through chapter 19 as far as verses 13 and 14. These are comprised of 22 words and 17 words respectively, highlighting exactly the same numbers as those dominant earlier. Once again, they feature strongly—this time throughout the scene before Pilate and the crucifixion. There are 20 multiples of 17 in the consecutive verse combinations, including one total of 153. In addition there are 26 multiples of 11, and just to round everything off with the perfect mathematical symbolism, there are two combinations of 490—seventy times seven, the motif of forgiveness.

> 'Father, forgive them, for they know not what they do.'
>
> Luke 23:34[ESV]

JOHN
3:31-36
B S B

'The One who comes
from above is above all.
The one who is from the earth belongs to the earth
and speaks as one from the earth.
The One who comes from heaven is above all.
He testifies to what He has seen and heard,
yet no one accepts His testimony. Whoever accepts
His testimony has certified that God is truthful.
For the One whom God has sent speaks the words
of God, for God gives the Spirit without limit.

The Father loves the Son and has placed all things
in His hands. Whoever believes in the Son has eternal life.
Whoever rejects the Son will not see life.
Instead, the wrath of God
remains on him.'

JOHN 19:13-15
BSB

When Pilate heard this,
he brought Jesus out and sat down on the
judge's seat at a place known as the Stone Pavement
(which in Aramaic is Gabbatha). It was the day
of Preparation of the Passover; it was about noon.

'Here is your king,' Pilate said to the Jews.

But they shouted,
'Take him away! Take him away! Crucify him!'

'Shall I crucify your king?' Pilate asked.

'We have no king but Caesar,'
the chief priests answered.

8.1 Earthly and Heavenly

> *'The One who comes from above is above all. The one who is from the earth belongs to the earth and speaks as one from the earth. The One who comes from heaven is above all. He testifies to what He has seen and heard, yet no one accepts His testimony.'*
>
> John 3:31–32[BSB]

> *When Pilate heard this, he brought Jesus out and sat down on the judge's seat at a place known as the Stone Pavement (which in Aramaic is Gabbatha). It was the day of Preparation of the Passover; it was about noon.*
>
> John 19:13–14[BSB]

It's unclear if these verses from the third chapter are direct speech from John the Baptiser or John the apostle's own comment. If it's the Baptiser then he is encouraging his own disciples to see that he is merely the King's herald, not the King Himself. He testifies that Jesus is the King of the World come down from heaven, compared to himself as merely an earth-birthed human.

In first-century Jewish thought, the world was divided three ways, and perhaps the threefold mention of *earth* subtly alludes to this. The three divisions of the world were considered to be: Jew, Samaritan and Gentile. To be King of the World and therefore qualified to be its Redeemer, Jesus has to have been declared as a king, or its equivalent, by all three groups.

Throughout his gospel record, John the apostle has carefully testified to the three different occasions when this requirement was fulfilled. The events following the meeting of Jesus with the woman at the well in Sychar fulfil the Samaritan third of this criteria,[180] the anointing of Jesus by Mary of Bethany—followed by the triumphal procession of Jesus into Jerusalem[181]—accomplishes the Jewish component; and now, seated on a judge's throne, Pilate is about to publicly complete that last necessary section. He is the Gentile who, in a judicial hearing, deems that Jesus is rightfully entitled to be called *king*.

Whether it's John the Baptiser or John the apostle who compares the One from heaven and the one from earth, the threefold mention of 'earth' reinforces our unworthiness as children of Adam in relation to Jesus. The Baptiser has already testified he is not worthy to untie the sandal of Jesus, the 'Lamb of God'. If these are his words, he's pointing his own disciples to Jesus as having come down from heaven. In contrast to those born of earth, Jesus is the One already 'born from above' who, through His death, will share the new birth with every believer.

If, on the other hand, this is a remark of John the apostle, then it's another strike against the Gnostic belief in the duality of the divine Son as Jesus the man co-mingled with Christ the divine spirit. Gnosticism denied the bodily incarnation of the Son as well as His death on the Cross. A Christ-spirit was said to descended on Jesus at His baptism and to have left Him before He was nailed

---

[180] The next book in this series, *The Inviolable Kingdom*, will outline how Jesus in Samaria brought about the reunification of the kingdom that had been torn apart after Solomon's death in the very place where the division occurred.

[181] John does not describe this procession, obviously relying on the knowledge of his readers regarding the other gospels.

to the Cross. Consequently salvation by grace through faith in the atonement for the forgiveness of sins was impossible—God had not died, only man had.

For the Gnostics, salvation was through knowledge. A fusion of Christian, Platonic, Pythagorean and other pagan ideas, Gnosticism offered its initiates secret wisdom devoid of righteous living.[182] Since only the spirit had value, not the body, then indulgence in sin didn't particularly matter. The temptation of this teaching is obvious, and new believers were led astray sometimes by the licence to surrender to the cravings of the flesh and sometimes by a sense of inferiority. The mystery religions had a hierarchy and various degrees of initiation and it no doubt seemed to some Gentile converts that Christianity was too simple and that they were being quietly excluded from the 'higher secrets'.

Yet John records that there are no higher secrets. There is belief in Jesus, or rejection of Jesus, and that's it. Jesus Himself proclaimed this but *'no one accepts His testimony.'* Through faith in Jesus, we come into covenantal relationship with Him—the oneness, the union, the concord of Bridegroom and Bride.

Here in the chiasmus, we have a curious allusion to that covenantal connection. The stone pavement where Pilate sat for judgment was in a colonnade, a paved inner court open to the sky. That is the original definition of a modern patio, derived from 'pascisci', Latin for *to covenant, to make a treaty*. The Roman sense of colonnade thus apparently had an inbuilt notion of a place to make or ratify covenants. Pilate's own name has some resonances of a colonnade—not in the sense of marble pillars but of heavy timber piles.[183]

---

182 There were, however, some forms of Gnosticism that were very ascetic and denied the flesh.
183 See: etymonline.com/search?q=pilum (accessed 25 April 2024) Pilate's name is thought to derive from 'pilum' and mean *javelin*. However 'pilum' also refers to *heavy timber beams* driven into the ground for structural support.

John describes the pavement as 'lithostrōtos', *a tessellated stone area*, known in Aramaic as 'Gabbatha'. It is thought that Gabbatha is derived from 'gibeah', *ridge* or *hill*, and 'beit', *house*—and thus refers to an elevated place near the Temple. He mentions that this was the Day of Preparation of the Passover. And so his word-combination evokes echoes of a long-gone much-overlooked Passover sacrifice that involved a breach of covenant. Here we have a recapitulation of a horrific covenant betrayal in the time of David.

In Hebrew the word for *tessellated pavement* is 'rizpah'. An alternative word for 'gibeah' with the same meaning is Gibeon, the city that, in the time of David, was the site of the tent that housed the Tabernacle. It was the hill of the house of God.

During a famine, David inquired of the Lord as to the cause and was told it was because Saul had broken covenant and killed the Gibeonites. David therefore inquired of the Gibeonites what they wanted to bless the land. Their reply eerily foreshadows the almost identical words of the Jewish leaders appealing to Pilate:

It's not for us to execute anyone in Israel.	*We are not permitted to execute anyone.*
2 Samuel 21:4[ISV]	John 18:31[NKJV]

Just as the Gibeonites were legally restricted from sentencing anyone to death, so too were the first-century Jews by the Romans. The Gibeonites sought permission for human sacrifice from David who was, for them, a foreign overlord.

- They killed their victims at the beginning of the barley harvest—Passover.
- Caiaphas, Annas and their supporters sought permission from Pilate, a foreign overlord, for human sacrifice at the Passover.

David, like Pilate, was weak and insecure—at least at that point in his reign when the land was devastated by drought. He agreed to hand over seven descendants of Saul to the Gibeonites, thereby breaching his multiple covenants with the House of Saul. The princes were slain and, instead of being honourably buried the same day, their bodies were exposed on the hill at Gibeon where the Tabernacle was situated. For months, everyone coming to pray for rain at the Tabernacle would have seen the massacred bodies and observed the lonely figure of Rizpah, the concubine of Saul,[184] who maintained a harrowing vigil trying to protect the bodies from further defilement by the elements or animals.

With just a few faint clues, John tells us that Jesus is in the midst of the process of recapitulating, mending, repairing, undoing David's horrendous covenant breach. Jesus walks through the same scenario to lift the defilement David brought on the land through his desperation to end the drought, his weakness in seeking to appease the Gibeonites rather than search out God's will, and his shrewd opportunism. Just as the chief priests were politically motivated to remove a threat to their power, so David was politically motivated to remove almost all[185] the threats to his throne from Saul's line.

John repeatedly allows us to catch glimpses of Jesus, the ultimate makeover artist, the supreme healer of history. He's the One above all—above all the patriarchs, prophets and kings. He's the One who handed Elijah's mantle to Simon Peter and Joseph's mantle to Mary Magdalene, Moses' mantle to Nicodemus and here he is,

---

184 She was apparently David's concubine as well, since God, in rebuking David for the affair with Bathsheba, says: *'I gave your master's house to you, and your master's wives into your arms. I gave you all Israel and Judah. And if all this had been too little, I would have given you even more.'* (2 Samuel 12:8[NIV])

185 The single exception was Jonathan's son, Meribaal, usually known as Mephibosheth, who was lame in both feet and therefore no threat to David's monarchy at all.

even in the midst of His trial, beginning His work of thoroughly cleansing David's mantle of the stain of covenant violation.

Covenant-keeping was David's strong point. It therefore became the area that was most under attack spiritually in his life and where he began to repeatedly fail. No wonder God says:

> *My power is perfected in weakness.*
>
> 2 Corinthians 12:10[BSB]

David's covenant breaches had brought great defilement on the nation. His own relationship with God had deteriorated over the years to the point where he was afraid of God and feared to go to the Tabernacle.[186] He continued to view God's favour towards him, even as the last song before his death attests, as evidence of his own righteousness rather than evidence of the love and grace of God.

This is a mistake all of us are apt to make. It's natural for us to believe that God will bless us if we're good and withdraw His approval and punish us if we're not. We tend to think His gifts depend on our righteous behaviour. Yet the offices and gifts of God are irrevocable—they wouldn't be *gifts* otherwise. Instead they'd be conditional grants.

We tend to judge leaders by their gifts, assuming that God would automatically remove the gift if they were secretly ungodly and corrupt. But because they're gifts, this doesn't happen. Jesus tells us we can recognise our true brothers and sisters in the faith by their fruit,[187] not by those immutable, unchangeable gifts God has given them that may be being used worthily or abused unworthily.

It's love, joy, peace, patience, kindness, goodness, faithfulness, gentleness and self-control that should form the basis of our discernment, not the gifts and talents God has showered on us.

---

186 1 Chronicles 21:29–30
187 Matthew 7:20

8.2 Rejection

Whoever accepts His testimony has certified that God is truthful. For the One whom God has sent speaks the words of God, for God gives the Spirit without limit.

The Father loves the Son and has placed all things in His hands. Whoever believes in the Son has eternal life. Whoever rejects the Son will not see life. Instead, the wrath of God remains on him.

John 3:33–36^{BSB}

'Here is your king,' Pilate said to the Jews.

But they shouted, 'Take Him away! Take Him away! Crucify Him!'

'Shall I crucify your king?' Pilate asked.

'We have no king but Caesar,' the chief priests answered.

John 19:14–15^{BSB}

IN THE DAYS OF THE PROPHET SAMUEL, when it became clear that his sons did not take after him but rather after the corrupt priests preceding him, the people of Israel demanded a king.

And the Lord told him: 'Listen to all that the people are saying to you; it is not you they have rejected, but they have rejected Me as their king.'

1 Samuel 8:7^{NIV}

Over a millennium later, after a long and consistent spurning of God, the Jewish leaders of the first century—the chief priests and the majority of the ruling Sanhedrin—finally took the ultimate step. They rejected Jesus, the Son of God, in favour of Tiberius, 'divi filius', *son of god*. Like Augustus before him, Tiberius was an adopted son and furthered his claim to legitimacy through the title, *son of god*, meaning 'adopted son of the deified father'.[188]

The non-acceptance of Jesus as the Messiah by Annas and Caiaphas is actually immaterial at this point. Their statement, *'We have no king but Caesar,'* is an utterly blasphemous affront to the Most High God. It wasn't an out-of-character new step. They were already steeped in blasphemy—they were the ones, after all, who insisted the Temple tax could only be paid with a silver half-shekel adorned with a graven image of Herakles-Melkart, the god of death.[189] Yet here they've taken the age-old rejection of God as king by their forbears to a whole new level of offence and sacrilege. To choose Caesar as king in a place where covenants are ratified is to pledge allegiance, generation upon generation, to the rulers of Rome. Furthermore it is to forfeit the protection of God by breaching covenant with Him. Even if they had not demanded the death of Jesus at this point, nothing short of national repentance could have saved them from a Roman invasion. But they did take their responsibility further:

> *'His blood be on us and on our children!'*
>
> Matthew 27:25[ESV]

---

188   Augustus first used the title 'divi filius', *son of god*, after his adopted father Julius Caesar was divinised following his death. Likewise, Augustus was divinised after death, so Tiberius could then easily lay claim to the same title. He is thought to have refused the title but it was still in common usage.

189   See: *The Summoning of Time: John 2 and 20*, the second book in this series.

Having thus called the Avenger of Blood upon themselves and their children, they could not expect more than a generation's grace. They destroyed a holy Temple—the body of Jesus—so inevitably they reaped the destruction of their own holy Temple in Jerusalem.

Just as the people came out from under God's covenantal protection during the Baal-Peor incident and tens of thousands died, so now—having declined God's defence—hundreds of thousands would die in the war with the imperial legions. The son of god from Rome would come to claim his own[190] and punish those who rejected his rule.

John is very clear in this section. He's writing after the destruction of Jerusalem and he's unequivocally declaring: *'The Father loves the Son and has placed all things in His hands.'* Nothing has happened that is beyond the oversight of the true Son of God, Jesus the Lord of Heaven and Earth.

The emperors Vespasian and Titus—both deceased and deified by the time John was putting this down in his record—might have destroyed Galilee and Judea, even razing the Temple, but this too was foreseen. Those who believe in Jesus are not outside His keeping power. He warned His followers to leave Jerusalem as soon as they saw the besieging armies—and, taking Him at His word, many of them fled to Pella.

On the other hand, Jesus will take those who decline His offer of salvation at their word—if they don't want to be saved, He won't save them. Simple as that.

---

190 Vespasian was deified on his death. Titus, his son, sacked Jerusalem and was also divinised on his death by his brother Domitian who then claimed to be a living god. It was during the time of Domitian that John was writing his gospel.

> *Whoever believes in the Son has eternal life. Whoever rejects the Son will not see life. Instead, the wrath of God remains on him.*
>
> John 3:36^{BSB}

God is love.

One aspect of that love is to grant us freewill and never override it. He will stand in harm's way for us for a time—sometimes even a very long time—but ultimately, if we choose another god, He will allow our choice to stand and leave us to the consequences of that choice. The leaders of the Jewish people in the first century were given a generation to return to God as king.

The high priest Caiaphas had been the instrument to bring about the murder of an innocent man, violating all the laws of the judiciary as well as the commandments of God in order to gain the conviction he wanted. A generation later, the reaping began. The high priest Jonathan was murdered by the 'sicarii', the earliest known band of assassins. These were a group within the zealots who wanted war, whatever the cost. They were the ones who burned the stores of grain Nicodemus and his friends had stockpiled in order that all the citizens of Jerusalem could survive a prolonged siege. The 'sicarii' were named for the 'sicae' or small concealable daggers they wore. Spreading terror by knifing anyone suspected of being a Roman sympathiser, they kidnapped the secretary of Eleazar, the governor of the Temple precincts, and agreed to release him in exchange for ten captured assassins.[191] They are also thought to have murdered Nicodemus' brother.

Now, at this point in his narrative, John leaves out a significant detail. He omits any mention of Pilate washing his hands. This

---

191 A similarly uneven exchange ratio seems to have been adopted by Hamas militants and the Israeli government during the negotiations for release of hostages from Gaza who were taken during the 7 October 2023 incursion.

seeming oversight is curious—since, after all, John is supreme amongst the early church writers for his references to water. Was he, once again, relying on the familiarity of his readers with the other gospels? Possibly.

However, the most likely reason for not remarking on Pilate washing his hands is because he was not using *lustral* water. His washing was not an act symbolic of purification or repentance. Rather it was to disclaim responsibility, to proclaim innocence, to shift blame and negate shame.

The act of repentance takes on board responsibility for wrongdoing and, while it can't undo the past, it assumes a resolve to change the future. It is motivated by a desire to turn away from sin and, empowered by God, to avoid repeating it. Repentance, while it can't undo, ideally involves restitution.

Pilate's declaration has a marked similarity to the believers of today who, on becoming aware of the sowing-and-reaping principle and realising the consequences of their past actions, decide to decree those unwelcome outcomes away and to declare agreeable ones instead. They don't want to change their behaviour or admit that they are treating others in a way they do not care to suffer themselves, they simply want the consequences washed away. And so it is that God's grace-gift of repentance is disdained in favour of a prophetic declaration that attempts to sidle around it. Responsibility, however, is not so easily bypassed.

8.3 Living and Lustral

Lustral waters are, by definition, purifying and sanctifying.[192] The word 'lustral' is tangentially related to *lustre*, and thus it has a resonance suggesting a surface that is overlaid and shimmering with light. The radiant beauty of lustral waters dance with life, reminding us of the living waters of the Holy Spirit.

So it should not be in any way surprising that John, in his upcoming fourth chapter, continues to flow with his theme of water—living water that refreshes and quenches our soul-deep thirst for Spirit and truth.

He is, of course, about to disclose another significant mantle and to describe the occasion when Jesus handed it on to His first evangelist. This time it's a royal mantle under consideration. That's the reason living water is so important to the storyline as recorded in the next chapter: because *living* water had long been an essential ceremonial element for the coronation of a king.

---

192 'Lustral' also has the sense of 'once every five years'.

APPENDIX I:
Word and Letter Count[193]

Verse	Words	Letters	Verse	Words	Letters
John 3:1	12	60	John 3:19	28	109
John 3:2	32	140 or 141	John 3:20	20	74
John 3:3	21	95	John 3:21	19	80
John 3:4	23	125	John 3:22	20	92
John 3:5	**22** or 23	105 or 106	John 3:23	20	90 or 91
John 3:6	15	76	John 3:24	8 or 9	38 or 39 or 40
John 3:7	9	44	John 3:25	11	61 or 62
John 3:8	26	120	John 3:26	27	125 or 127
John 3:9	9	52	John 3:27	**17**	84 or 86
John 3:10	15	69	John 3:28	18	91
John 3:11	18	88	John 3:29	30	123
John 3:12	15	69	John 3:30	6	34
John 3:13	**17**	72	John 3:31	28	110
John 3:14	16	70	John 3:32	12	65
John 3:15	9	35	John 3:33	11	52
John 3:16	25	109	John 3:34	**17**	68
John 3:17	21	82	John 3:35	12	47
John 3:18	**22** or 23	100 or 102	John 3:36	14	91

---

193 The text used for these counts is Greek NT: Westcott and Hort/[NA28]. Calculations always use the lowest alternative.

APPENDIX II:
Word and Letter Count[194]

The variations in the letter count in this section mainly concern the spelling of the name 'Pilate' in Greek—Pilatos or Peilatos.

Verse	Words	Letters	Verse	Words	Letters
John 19:13	22	116 or 117	John 19:28	15	68
John 19:14	17	69	John 19:29	15	88
John 19:15	24	133	John 19:30	16	76
John 19:16	11	59	John 19:31	35	158 or 159
John 19:17	15	82 or 83	John 19:32	17	82 or 83
John 19:18	15	75	John 19:33	15	68
John 19:19	21	100 or 101	John 19:34	15	72
John 19:20	25	130	John 19:35	20	100 or 101
John 19:21	20 or 21	97 or 98 or 104 or 105	John 19:36	11	57
			John 19:37	9	46
John 19:22	6	31 or 32	John 19:38	37 or 38	167 or 169 or 170
John 19:23	32	153			
John 19:24	35 or 37	175 or 183	John 19:39	19	87 or 88
John 19:25	24	99 or 100	John 19:40	19	97
John 19:26	19	79	John 19:41	20	82
John 19:27	20	77	John 19:42	15	69

---

194 The text used for these counts is Greek NT: Westcott and Hort/[NA28]. Calculations always use the lowest alternative.

OTHER BOOKS BY ANNE HAMILTON

STRATEGIES FOR THE THRESHOLD series

Dealing with Python: Spirit of Constriction (with Arpana Dev Sangamithra)
Dealing with Ziz: Spirit of Forgetting
Name Covenant: Invitation to Friendship
Hidden in the Cleft: True and False Refuge
Dealing with Leviathan: Spirit of Retaliation
Dealing with Resheph: Spirit of Trouble (with Irenie Senior)
Dealing with Azazel: Spirit of Rejection
Dealing with Belial: Spirit of Abuse and Armies (with Janice Speirs)
Dealing with Kronos: Spirit of Time and Abuse (with Janice Speirs)
Dealing with Lilith: Spirit of Dispossession
Dealing with Rachab: Spirit of Wasting

DEVOTIONAL THEOLOGY series

God's Poetry: The Identity & Destiny Encoded in Your Name
God's Panoply: The Armour of God & the Kiss of Heaven
God's Pageantry: The Threshold Guardians & the Covenant Defender
God's Pottery: The Sea of Names & the Pierced Inheritance
God's Priority: World-Mending & Generational Testing
More Precious than Pearls (with Natalie Tensen)
As Resplendent as Rubies (with Natalie Tensen)
As Exceptional as Sapphires (with Donna Ho)
Spiritual Legal Rights (with Janice Sergison)
Core Values: Love (with Rebekah Robinson)
Core Values: Joy (with Rebekah Robinson)
Core Values: Peace (with Rebekah Robinson)
Core Values: Patience (with Rebekah Robinson)

JESUS AND THE HEALING OF HISTORY series

Like Wildflowers, Suddenly
Bent World, Bright Wings
Silk Shadows, Rings of Gold
Where His Feet Pass
The Singing Silence
In the Meshes of the Net
Interpreted by Love

Grace Drops with Anne podcast: https://gracedropswithanne.com

This series begins in Volume 1:

ISBN 978-1-925380-53-8

The Elijah Tapestry is the first volume in an examination of the mirror-like chiastic patterning in the fourth gospel. John has designed his account of the life of Jesus as an epic poem in the style of Hebrew prophecy. This is demonstrated by aligning matching ideas at the beginning and end of the gospel.

As a result, a concealed theme is unveiled involving the passing of Elijah's mantle after the death of John the Baptiser. That legacy involves a divine assignment that has lain, dormant and unfinished, for nine centuries. Jesus, in reactivating the mantle, passes it to one of His disciples to carry on the work still to be fulfilled.

Volume 2:

ISBN 978-1-925380-75-0

The Summoning of Time is the second volume in an examination of the mirror-like chiastic patterning in John's gospel. Once again, the match of parallel segments brings to light another hidden message that John embedded in his narrative.

There's a tendency to consider that a mantle is passed so the recipient can repeat the good works of the original owner—whereas, in John's gospel, it becomes clear it is passed so the unfinished works of the owner can be completed. In the first and last chapters, John addresses the matter of Elijah's mantle. In the second and second-last chapters, he turns to Joseph's coat-of-many-colours and shows us where Jesus bestowed it.

The wedding at Cana, the chasing of the money-lenders from the Temple and the meeting with Mary Magdalene in the garden are aligned in corresponding sections to reveal Jesus' message about the coming of a new era and the summoning of time.

This series continues in Volume 4:

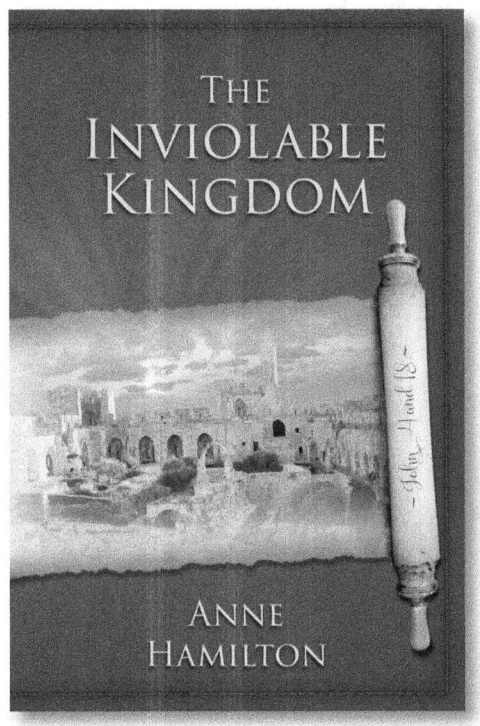

ISBN 978-1-925380-82-8

The Inviolable Kingdom is the fourth volume in an examination of the mirror-like chiastic patterning in John's gospel. Almost a millennium has passed since the united monarchy was ripped apart during the coronation week of Rehoboam, the grandson of David. Jesus returns to the very spot where it happened and, with nothing other than a simple request for water, He begins reunifying David's long-divided kingdom.

Once again, verses from the beginning of the gospel—chapter four this time—are paired with verses from the end. John is not only building a body of evidence for Jesus as the triply-proclaimed King of the World but also as the incomparable Healer of History.

www.ingramcontent.com/pod-product-compliance
Lightning Source LLC
Chambersburg PA
CBHW070655120526
44590CB00013BA/974